D0030007

POLARIZED

POLARIZED
The Rise of Ideology in American Politics

Steven E. Schier and Todd E. Eberly

ROWMAN & LITTLEFIELD
Lanham • Boulder • New York • London

Published by Rowman & Littlefield
A wholly owned subsidary of The Rowman & Littlefield Publishing Group, Inc.
4501 Forbes Boulevard, Suite 200, Lanham, Maryland 20706
www.rowman.com

Unit A, Whitacre Mews, 26-34 Stannary Street, London SE11 4AB

Copyright © 2016 by Rowman & Littlefield

All rights reserved. No part of this book may be reproduced in any form or by any
electronic or mechanical means, including information storage and retrieval systems,
without written permission from the publisher, except by a reviewer who may quote
passages in a review.

British Library Cataloguing in Publication Information Available

Library of Congress Cataloging-in-Publication Data

978-1-4422-5484-8 (cloth)
978-1-4422-5486-2 (paper)
978-1-4422-5485-5 (ebook)

∞™ The paper used in this publication meets the minimum requirements of
American National Standard for Information Sciences—Permanence of Paper
for Printed Library Materials, ANSI/NISO Z39.48-1992.

Printed in the United States of America

Contents

1

Ideology in American Politics

L IBERAL? MODERATE? CONSERVATIVE? In the media, these terms appear constantly, but what do they mean? Much of America's political discourse involves ideological labels. These labels are full of content, and explain the stakes of contemporary politics. They are signifiers of *ideology*, a concept defined by Webster's dictionary as "the integrated assertions, theories and aims that constitute a sociopolitical program" (Merriamwebster.com 2013). Ideology centers on beliefs and assumptions about society, politics, and culture. Specifically, it is, as defined above, a program for improving human politics, culture, and society. It is hardly surprising that ideology lies at the heart of contemporary controversies in American politics.

Defining Ideology

Ideology is a complex but important concept in social science. As political scientist John Gerring, a student of ideology, noted, "Few concepts in the social science lexicon have occasioned so much discussion, so much disagreement and so much self-conscious discussion of the disagreement, as 'ideology.' Condemned time and again for its . . . unclarity, the concept of ideology remains, against all odds, a central term of social science research" (Gerring 1997, 357–59). S. L. C. Destutt de Tracy coined the term in 1817 as a brief description of the "science of ideas" (Eysenick and Wilson 1978a). The term gradually came to be widely employed by philosophers and social theorists in the nineteenth and twentieth centuries, such as Karl Marx, Georg Hegel,

Sigmund Freud, Karl Mannheim, Pierre Bourdieu, and Claude Lévi-Strauss. Along the way, it accumulated a rather complex definition. Hans Eysenick and Glenn Wilson defined its five characteristics deriving from decades of theoretical development. Ideology (1) contains an explanatory theory of human experience, (2) sets out a program for social and political organization, (3) conceives of the program's attainment as requiring a struggle, (4) seeks loyal adherents, and (5) addresses a wide public but may confer leadership upon intellectuals (Eysenick and Wilson 1978b, 305).

That is a long list of features, and most, if not all of them, are evident in contemporary American liberalism and conservatism. Each has their own explanation of their cause, agenda for action, perception of ideological opponents, loyal followers, and intellectual leaders. In subsequent chapters, we explore these several facets of liberalism and conservatism and their impact upon America's political system.

Here we use a definition of ideology that is a bit less elaborate than the one widely employed in social science and closer to the short definition with which we began the chapter. Political scientists William Flanigan and Nancy Zingale provide a cogent definition: "A *political ideology* is a set of fundamental beliefs or principles about politics and government: what the scope of government should be; how decisions should be made; what values should be pursued" (Flanigan and Zingale 2010, 135). That is short, but expansive as well. Ideology concerns the grand issues of politics.

Ideology in the American Media

The media regularly employ ideological labels in discussing politics. Consider the following examples. *New York Times* blogger Thomas Edsall, an experienced political reporter and analyst, recently addressed the challenges facing liberalism: "Liberalism now faces the job of paying for its own success in helping people to live longer. The progressive ethos, currently embattled, has a proud history. What is uncertain is whether a durable social consensus can be mobilized in the face of global economic pressure to reduce taxes and limit the scope of government" (Edsall 2013). Edsall uses "progressive" as a synonym for "liberal" and we also do that in this book.

The label of "moderates" gets steady media usage as well. Former Republican senator John Danforth discussed that perspective in a column on religion and politics: "It is important for those of us who are sometimes called moderates to make the case that we, too, have strongly held Christian convictions, that we speak from the depths of our beliefs, and that our approach to politics is at least as faithful as that of those who are more conservative" (Danforth

2005). As Danforth's statement suggests, moderates commonly are placed between liberals and conservatives on the political spectrum. The many disagreements between liberals and conservatives give moderates much space in which to locate themselves between the liberal and conservative poles of opinion.

In recent decades, each of the nation's two major political parties increasingly have become defined by their ideological orientations. Simply put, nowadays more Democrats are liberals and more Republicans conservatives. A recent Associated Press story regarding the GOP-majority in the US House reflects the growing ideological uniformity of the parties: "House Republicans flexed their cultural and conservative muscles Tuesday, passing the most restrictive abortion measure in years. They also advanced legislation to crack down on immigrants living illegally in the country" (Associated Press 2013).

This last example illustrates how much media coverage of parties and ideology in national politics includes specific content about issue positions. The statement notes how Republican Representatives are strongly antiabortion and prefer a strict approach to changes in immigration laws. Democrats and liberals, in contrast, are much more likely to favor abortion rights and more permissive immigration reforms. But those two issue differences are just the tip of the ideological iceberg of differences separating liberals and conservatives.

Defining Liberalism and Conservatism

Table 1.1 contains a roster of major differences between contemporary American liberalism and conservatism. We can understand those dissimilarities as deriving from two contrasting beliefs. First, liberals tend to view America's problems as centering upon undeserved inequalities among its citizens. Differences in incomes and opportunities between the rich and poor, men and women, gays and straights, and whites and racial minorities are central political problems deserving reform. Conservatives, in contrast, adopt individual liberty as a primary value. Ever-growing government threatens individual freedom to operate businesses, follow religious convictions, speak freely, and own firearms. For them, protection of such liberties ranks as a top priority.

Second, liberals believe government, often the national government, should take action to address the inequalities they see as plaguing American society. Liberals applaud the considerable increase in the size of the national government over the last one hundred years as national programs appeared providing income support, health care, environmental protection, and business regulation. Conservatives, in contrast, believe government is now too large and has failed to solve many of the problems it has spent billions of

TABLE 1.1

Differences Between Contemporary U.S. Liberalism and Conservatism

Liberalism	Conservatism
Equality the most important value	Liberty the most important value
Favors extensive government intervention in the economy	Views large government as threat to individual freedom
Favors expansion of federal social services	Suspicious of governmental expansion of social and economic interventions
For more governmental efforts on behalf of the poor, minorities and women	Prefers private-sector solutions for the disadvantaged
Favors national government as an instigator of policy change	Favors state and local governmental initiatives over national efforts
Supports enhanced environmental protection, abortion rights, gay marriage	Opposes abortion, gay marriage, supports school prayer
Supports nuclear arms control	Favors maintenance of U.S. military power
Favors more aid for poor nations and international organizations	Supports U.S. national interests as a guide to foreign affairs
Challenges the social, economic, and cultural values of the business and commercial strata	Defends traditional social institutions and businesses from challenges by organized labor, minorities, intellectuals, and some professionals

Source: derived from Theodore Lowi, Benjamin Ginsberg, Kenneth Shepsle, and Stephen Ansolabehere, *American Government: Power and Purpose* (New York: Norton, 2012), 409–11.

dollars addressing. Some governmental actions, they argue, have made the economy more inefficient and thus lowered the nation's standard of living.

Liberals and conservatives also disagree about which levels of government are most likely to solve the key American problems. Liberals hold that many of the issues on their agenda concern national problems requiring national solutions. Conservatives believe that smaller, lower levels of government—states, counties, and cities—can act more responsibly and efficiently in addressing problems. This is a disagreement about *federalism*, the arrangement of powers between a county's national, state, and local governments. American federalism is often celebrated by conservatives and decried as an obstacle to necessary reforms by liberals.

On international issues, liberals believe America should take the lead in addressing a series of international social, environmental, and economic problems. Global economic inequality, international arms proliferation, and world environmental challenges, they argue, demand US leadership in a collaborative matter in international institutions such as the United Nations. Conservatives tend to view America's international role in terms of the country's national interests and military might. They cast a skeptical eye on schemes of international improvement, just as they are suspicious of expansive reform programs by national government in domestic affairs.

Not all liberals and conservatives agree on every issue. One can identify factions within these broad orientations, and we do so later in this chapter. One group of conservatives, for example, is the "libertarians," who particularly emphasize individual freedom and small government. Some libertarians diverge from social conservatives on issues such as abortion, individual drug use, and gay marriage. Libertarians tend to view these issues as individual rights that should be free from governmental restrictions. Social conservatives, however, view limitations on abortion, gay marriage, and drug use as essential for the moral health of American society. Liberals also have their internal disagreements. Some of the most progressive liberals seek a drastic reduction in national military spending and intelligence gathering, but other liberals view these as essential to national security. Liberals also at times disagree about specific sorts of environmental protection and economic and social policies.

And the moderates? Where are they? They scatter between the two poles of America's ideological spectrum. There are, however, some identifiable types of moderates in contemporary politics. One sort is the economic conservative/social liberal. Similar to the libertarians mentioned above, these moderates are political independents, not identifying with either major party. They are skeptical of governmental intervention in the economy yet share many liberals' support of social changes such as abortion rights, gay marriage, and drug legalization. Why are they not Republicans? A strong aversion to social conservatives has moved many of them out of the GOP and into the moderate independent category. Younger and higher-income Americans, as chapter 2 reveals, populate the economic conservative/social liberal category.

Another moderate type is the economic liberal/social conservative citizen. These people tend to be lower in education and income, finding attractive the liberals' economic policies combating inequality. Many, however, are religious and hold to traditional views opposing abortion, gay marriage, and drug legalization. Though ideologically moderate, many of these voters choose Democratic candidates in the polling booth for economic reasons. That is one reason why Democrats have a higher proportion of moderates in their ranks than do Republicans, as we note in the next section. Many African Americans are in this ideological group.

Ideology, Partisanship, and Polarization

At the outset, it is important to note some basic contours of ideology among the American public. We will do this by discussing its relationship to two central political characteristics: partisanship and polarization. In recent decades, the two major political parties have become more ideologically homogeneous—Democrats more uniformly liberal, Republicans more uniformly conservative. We can examine this by presenting survey evidence regarding partisan and ideological self-identification—which party and ideological labels survey respondents adopt over time.

Since the 1970s, the two major parties have increased their ideological uniformity. This is particularly the case among Republicans. From 1974–1980, the percentage of GOPers identifying themselves as conservatives averaged 47 percent and the proportion labeling themselves as liberals averaged 19 percent. From 2002–2012, those averages had shifted to 67 percent conservative and a tiny 8 percent liberal, making the GOP more uniformly a party of self-identified conservatives. Democrats also shifted in a liberal direction from the 1970s to the present. From 1974–1989, the party averaged 33 percent self-identified liberals and 25 percent self-identified conservatives. From 2002–2012, those averages shifted to 38 percent liberal and only 18 percent conservative (General Social Survey 1974–1980, 2002–2012). Democrats from 2002–2012 had more moderates in their ranks—45 percent, compared to 26 percent for Republicans. Among those partisans who are most politically active, the ideological self-label is on average located more toward the extreme end of the ideological spectrum, as noted further in chapter 2.

Political polarization has two characteristics. First, those who are politically active must divide strongly on many major issues before the country. Second, within the major parties, its activists must hold relatively uniform issue positions. Those two traits describe American politics today.

Those who pay attention and are politically active dominate politics. In our two major parties, those who hold sway are strongly liberal Democrats and strongly conservative Republicans. Thus, the parties polarize over all manner of contemporary issues: gay marriage (Dems for, GOP against), welfare spending (Dems for, GOP against), abortion restrictions (Dems against, GOP for), some forms of gun control (Dems for, GOP against), tax increases (Dems for, GOP against), and spending cuts (GOP for, Dems against). The list could go on and on.

The evidence on this is unambiguous. In 2013, 59 percent of Democrats but only 29 percent of Republicans approved of gay marriage (Pew Forum 2013). Eighty percent of GOPers but only 48 percent of Democrats thought it was important for America to be the world's number-one military power (Newport 2013a). Fifty-nine percent of Democrats but only 33 percent of Republicans thought too little is spent on the environment (Newport 2013b). Democrats favored an assault weapons ban by 68 percent compared to only 39 percent of Republicans (Pew Research Center 2013). Seventy-two percent of Republicans in 2012 chose reducing the federal debt as a priority over more spending to stimulate the economy; 63 percent of Democrats preferred more spending (Pew Research Center 2012). Is too much spent on welfare for the poor? In 2012, 59 percent of Republicans agreed with that, but only 33 percent of Democrats did (General Social Survey 2012). Among Democrats, 61 percent approved of legalized abortion for "any reason" but only 31 percent of Republicans held that position (Pew Research Center 2012). Fifty-nine percent of Democrats favored legalizing marijuana but only 36 percent of Republican concurred (General Social Survey 2012).

Political scientist Morris Fiorina summarizes the consequences of America's current partisan polarization:

> [T]hose most active in politics—the political class, including convention delegates, donors and campaign activists—have indeed become more polarized since the 1970s. And the partisan media and many of the myriad groups dedicated to a single cause did not even exist a generation ago. As a general observation, the higher up the scale of political activity one goes, the more common extreme views become and the more intensely they are held: there are few "raging moderates" or "knee-jerk independents" at the higher levels of politics. Although relatively few in number, those in the political class structure politics. (Fiorina 2013)

It is clear that ideological differences between our two major parties lie at the center of American politics. Understanding ideology's characteristics is a key to grasping the present and future course of national politics. We next turn to those attributes, their uses by individuals, and their public utility in politics.

John Gerring holds that ideology has three main traits: internal coherence, external contrast, and stability. First, a set of values and beliefs must be internally coherent in order to be "ideological." This coherence, perceived in the mind of the person holding such views, serves to restrict or constrain the judgments and actions of the individual. Liberals refuse to support conservative causes and conservatives will not vote for liberal candidates. Second, "internal coherence implies a degree of contrast between the ideology in question and surrounding ideologies. . . . A value, belief or attitude is ideological only in reference to something else which it is not" (Gerring 1997, 974). Liberals and conservatives are quite aware of contrasting ideological ideas and can spot them readily. Third, "a set of values or beliefs must endure for some length of time in order to warrant the appellation 'ideology' . . . Frequent and repeated changes of political perspective, in other words, are usually considered good evidence of a lack of ideological commitment" (Gerring 1997, 975). Liberals and conservatives often derisively label moderates "squishy" because they are less constrained by ideological commitments in their thoughts and actions.

The Utility of Ideology for Individuals and Leaders

Individuals who develop ideological orientations find them a very useful way to order their political thoughts and actions. Once one couples ideological commitments with knowledge of current issues and political leaders, the appropriate direction and scope of political activity becomes easy to assess. It follows that those more highly educated tend to have more knowledge about politics and to be more prone to ideological thinking. Such individuals are more likely to have encountered abstract ideological concepts and to have applied them to the political world. Personal ideology becomes a handy conceptual shorthand for understanding politics.

Given that many citizens do think ideologically and order their political behavior according to their ideological thinking, political leaders have resorted to explicit ideological appeals. The ideologically liberal Barack Obama often discusses the need for increased governmental programs regarding the environment, economy, and society in terms used by his fellow liberals. Liberal programmatic appeals comprised much of the president's 2013 State of the Union Address:

> It is our unfinished task to make sure that this government works on behalf of the many, and not just the few. . . . We won't grow the middle class simply by shifting the cost of health care or college onto families that are already struggling, or by forcing communities to lay off more teachers and more cops and more firefighters. . . . for the sake of our children and our future, we must do more to combat climate change. . . . Tonight, let's declare that in the wealthiest nation on Earth, no one who works full-time should have to live in poverty, and raise the federal minimum wage to $9.00 an hour. (*New York Times* 2013a)

In contrast, 2012 GOP presidential nominee Mitt Romney described himself as a "severe conservative" and ideological appeals were a staple of his rhetoric. In his 2012 acceptance speech at the Republican National convention, for example, he touted the free enterprise system and criticized government attempts to make incomes more equal: "Business and growing jobs is about taking risk, sometimes failing, sometimes succeeding, but always striving. . . . It's the genius of the American free enterprise system—to harness the extraordinary creativity and talent and industry of the American people with a system that is dedicated to creating tomorrow's prosperity rather than trying to redistribute today's" (Fox News 2012).

How do leaders benefit from their ideological appeals? For one thing, they motivate their partisan and ideological followers to action—contributing money, volunteering for the campaign, and sending out supportive messages in social media. We noted earlier in this chapter how those more active politically are also more ideological. Second, leaders' ideological appeals seek to win converts to the cause by couching an agenda in attractive and appealing language.

President Obama pursued both goals when rallying Florida supporters in 2013 by criticizing Republicans for wrongheaded ideological priorities:

> [W]hen you get to the point where you've got another party that is more inter-ested in trying to roll back health care for 30 million Americans than provide health care for 30 million Americans; when you have a party that is trying to roll back Wall Street reform . . . instead of trying to implement it so that we don't have another batch of Wall Street bailouts; when you have a situation where folks are trying to make sure that women don't have the capacity to choose health care for themselves and make their own health care decisions . . . when folks aren't interested in compromising, then I want to make sure that I've got people there who are ready to do some work. (Whitehouse.gov 2013a)

During his 2012 campaign, Mitt Romney employed similar ideological ap-peals in rallying his backers at the Conservative Political Action Conference:

> Politicians are routinely elected on promises to change Washington, but when they come here, they become creatures of Washington. They begin to see gov-ernment as the answer to every challenge and the solution for every problem. At every turn, they try to substitute the heavy hand of the federal government for free citizens and free enterprise. They think government knows better—and can do better—than a free people exercising their free will. And this President is the worst offender. Barack Obama is the poster child for the arrogance of govern-ment. (*New York Times* 2013b)

Ideology creates a circular relationship between leaders and followers. By speaking ideologically, leaders reinforce ideological thinking among citi-zens, who then are encouraged to employ ideology as a way of guiding their thoughts and actions in the political world. A more educated population is more suited to operating according to ideological abstractions. So the great ideological divide, now represented well by America's two major parties, continues across time. With education levels increasing, more citizens under-stand ideological abstractions. America's political language and contests are likely to grow more ideological in coming years.

Foundations of Liberalism and Conservatism

What are the central animating principles of contemporary American liberal-ism and conservatism? Political scientist Martin Marietta describes the cen-tral conservative goal as the pursuit of "ordered liberty," defined as "freedom with decency, or liberty without license" (Marietta 2012, 21). Conservatives, he argues, view freedom as the ultimate good but are not optimistic about human nature and human potential. As a result, alongside liberty must be a public culture bolstering the traditional values of personal responsibility and self-restraint. Social conservatives tend to place top priority on the proper moral "order" while libertarian conservatives emphasize "liberty" as the primary good.

Underlying this conservative prescription are a series of assumptions. First, human societies are fragile and tend to degenerate over time, often due to selfishness and moral degeneracy. This is because human nature is at root flawed—"self-seeking, combative, and potentially aggressive" (Marietta 2012, 17). So one should give up utopian visions of a perfect world achievable by conscious human efforts. The utopian impulse leads to the destruction of freedom, as it did in communist regimes such as the Soviet Union and its puppet states in East Europe and in militarist Japan, fascist Italy, and Nazi Germany. "The utopian impulse always leads to oppression and violence, because dissent will rise and dissent must then be destroyed in order to maintain unity and control" (Marietta 2012, 18).

Public enemy number one for most conservatives, then, is expanding and ambitious government. Given flawed human beings, the more powerful the government, the greater the abuses to individual rights. Though social conservatives want government to restrict certain practices such as abortion, they join with libertarian conservatives in seeking a smaller government that taxes less, spends less, and regulates less.

Liberals view government much more favorably than do conservatives. For them, the ultimate goal is social justice in the form of greater equality among citizens. The centrality of this goal derives from liberals' assumption that both humans and human society can be perfected through conscious effort, including the collective effort of government action (Marietta 2012, 44). Liberals are much less likely than conservatives to view human nature as having fixed and immutable qualities. Humans instead are malleable products of their environment. By altering that environment, human behavior—individually and collectively—can be improved.

Since great prospects for human betterment exist through collective action, liberals hold that government should be at the forefront in pursuing such progress. They view much twentieth-century legislation, such as the institution of Social Security, a government-managed retirement system, and civil rights laws forbidding racial discrimination, as great advances resulting from enlightened government. Progress, for liberals is an unending process, and governmental activism to ensure progress also must be unending. Each generation has its own progressive agenda. In the 1930s, it was economic relief; in the 1960s, civil rights for racial minorities; today, expanded rights for gays, lesbians, bisexuals, and transgendered individuals. Some liberal goals persist across time, particularly the need for more equal social and economic outcomes in order to make progress toward a more just society.

A related liberal belief is that we should not assume there are absolute truths about human nature of the sort asserted by conservatives. Instead, "we have to grant each perspective its own share of respect." The value this leads to is tolerance, "the acceptance of multiple views in a non-judgmental atmosphere" (Marietta 2012, 47). Just as conservatives chide liberals for readily abandoning traditional institutions, liberals criticize conservatives for an intolerant resistance to new cultural and social arrangements. Tolerance, for liberals, focuses upon increasing public acceptance of their progressive agenda.

Ordered liberty or social justice? That is a big choice between hugely contrasting goals. As we will see in later chapters, Americans divide over this choice, producing enduring ideological conflict at the heart of American politics.

One common set of labels for liberal and conservative differences involves the directions "left" and "right." Liberals reside on the left side of political opinion and conservatives on the right. Why? The terms "left" and "right" appeared during the French Revolution of 1789. Members of the National Assembly divided into supporters of the king to the Assembly president's right and supporters of the revolution to his left. One deputy, the Baron de Gauville, explained: "We began to recognize each other: those who were loyal to religion and the king took up positions to the right of the chair so as to avoid the shouts, oaths, and indecencies that enjoyed free rein in the opposing camp." Since that time, in France the left parties have the label of the "parties of movement" and the right as "parties of order" (Gauchet 1996, 242–45). American liberals likewise view themselves as channels of progressive movement and American conservatives seek to maintain much of the nation's traditional economic, social, and political order.

The Coherence of Contemporary Liberalism and Conservatism

The animating principles of liberalism and conservatism are contrasting and clear. The application of those principles to contemporary policy issues, however, leads to some disagreements within the liberal and conservative camps. It also leads to some inconsistencies of approach within each ideological perspective. "On the liberal side, for example, what is the logical connection between opposition to U.S. government intervention in the affairs of foreign nations and calls for greater intervention in America's economy and society?

On the conservative side, what is the logical relationship between opposition to government regulation of business and support for a ban on abortion?" (Lowi et al. 2012, 411).

Two reasons account for inconsistencies of this sort. First, each ideological perspective involves a diverse coalition of interest groups. Liberals, for example, include noninterventionists in foreign affairs and organizations like organized labor that seek a larger role for national government in the economy. Conservatism includes groups like the U.S. Chamber of Commerce, focused on rolling back business regulations, and antiabortion groups, seeking increased regulation of abortion choices. Keeping a diverse coalition together requires that agenda flexibility triumph over logical consistency.

Even though each ideological camp advocates certain core principles, factions within each camp disagree on the application of those principles regarding particular public policies. For example, the liberal emphasis on social justice through greater equality produces a general skepticism toward operations of market capitalism. Markets produce unequal results, and curbing the bad social and political consequences of those outcomes is a central imperative of contemporary liberalism. This leads liberals to propose a wide variety of governmental solutions to problems of the marketplace. Frequent liberal priorities include business regulation to prevent pollution, abuse of workers, and corporate chicanery along with taxes on business and high-income individuals to fund assistance to low-income Americans.

But how equal is equal enough? Liberals often disagree about this. Some are in favor of much more regulation and redistribution than are others. President Obama, for example, frequently received complaints from strong liberals in Congress that he needed to propose more taxes on the wealthy and on business. Senator Sherrod Brown (D-Ohio) in 2013 criticized the president's plan to limit cost-of-living increases in Social Security benefits to senior citizens: "I think the president is wrong . . . we should increase taxes on the wealthiest of Americans and we shouldn't cut Social Security" (Torry and Wehrman 2013). Liberals thus disagree about the scale of their agenda for change.

Conservatives tend to coalesce around the need for economic liberty. For them, voluntary marketplace exchanges involving individuals and businesses produce efficient outcomes that over time produce a more prosperous society. The substantial growth in national government regulation of the economy in the twentieth century unifies conservatives in opposition to big government (Ferguson 2013). Conservatives divide, however, on the proper role of government in regulating certain lifestyle issues. Some conservatives, such as the National Organization for Marriage and National Right to Life Coalition, argue against the legal changes permitting gay marriage and abortion. Libertarian conservatives, in contrast, accept such changes as a desirable expansion of individual choice and liberty.

Consider these diverging perspectives among conservatives regarding gay marriage. Brian Brown, president of the National Association for Marriage: "[C]ultures throughout human history have shared that marriage is the union of a man and a woman, and that this is a unique and special union—there's something unique about men and women, there's something unique about marriage between men and women, that this union is important for society, important for children, is in the best interest of children" (Brown 2012). Ted Olson, Solicitor General—the Justice Department's top lawyer—for GOP President George W. Bush: "[E]liminating the right of individuals to marry a same-sex partner relegated those individuals to 'second class' citizenship, and told them, their families and their neighbors that their love and desire for a sanctioned marital partnership was not worthy of recognition" (Olson 2010).

Contrasting Ideological Perspectives in Contemporary Policy Debates

Though disagreements within liberal and conservative ranks are notable, they are the exception to the norm in public policy debates. On most issues, conservatives and liberals present unified, contrasting positions. Liberals stress progressive action for social justice and conservatives tout restriction of government and enhanced personal liberties. Arguments over three controversial policy areas demonstrate the ideological divisions in the debate.

The Affordable Care Act, President Obama's massive reform of the nation's health care system, has been subject to ideological contestation ever since the president proposed it. Supporters routinely tout it for providing more equal access to health care for all citizens. As President Obama stated in a 2013 White House speech: "Are you really prepared to say that 30 million Americans out there shouldn't have health insurance? Are you really prepared to say that's not a worthy goal? That's why we're going to keep fighting with everything we've got to secure that right, to make sure that every American gets the care that they need when they need it at a price that they can afford" (Whitehouse. gov 2013b). Opponents claim the act impedes the freedom of individuals and businesses to arrange affordable health care. GOP Vice Presidential nominee Paul Ryan told the 2012 Republican convention: "Obamacare comes to more than two thousand pages of rules, mandates, taxes, fees, and fines that have no place in a free country" (Newsday.com 2012).

The debate over climate change also pits liberal definitions of justice through governmental regulation against conservative preferences for economic freedom. President Obama: "Peace with justice means refusing to condemn our children to a harsher, less hospitable planet. The effort to slow climate change requires bold action" (Whitehouse.gov 2013c). Former GOP House Speaker John Boehner touted economic growth as a rival goal: "Why would you want to increase the cost of energy and kill more American jobs at a time when the American people are asking, 'Where are the jobs?'" (Gibson 2013).

Another issue dividing left and right is affirmative action, the use of racial and gender preferences in workplace hiring, promotion, and firing and in college admission. Princeton Professor Julian Zelizer touts affirmative action programs for their promotion of racial justice: "These programs have been a stunning success, slowly starting to repair the immense damage caused by the nation's history of racism." Repealing the programs would "set back the government's power to deal with racial problems" (Zelizer 2013). Opponents of affirmative action, such as Linda Chavez, who worked in Ronald Reagan's White House, argue that such preferences lead to unfair infringement on the rights of those not benefitting from such preferences: "People are not all endowed equally with the same talents, with the same interests, with the same desires and motivations. . . . This idea that you're somehow going to achieve . . . perfect representation of every ethnic, racial and gender group across the board, at all levels of society—the only way you could do that would be through a kind of authoritarian regime in which you squelched liberty" (National Public Radio 2012).

The Rise of Stable Partisan-Ideological Linkages

Differences between liberals and conservatives today appear stark because they overlap with partisan divisions between Democrats and Republicans. This overlap was much less the case in the mid-twentieth century. In the 1930s, 1940s, and 1950s, each major party was a "big tent" in which resided divergent ideological orientations. Democratic factions included a northern liberal wing, now dominant today, but also a group of white southern segregationists. The battle for civil rights for African Americans primarily occurred within the Democratic Party. Congressional Democrats then evidenced considerable disunity when voting on racial and social welfare legislation. The Republican Party of that time included a moderate wing of northeastern GOPers alongside a more conservative faction from the Midwest and mountain states. Congressional Republicans at times divided over labor and social welfare legislation.

Beginning in the 1960s, the two parties gradually became more ideologically uniform. Conservative southern whites gradually migrated from the Democrats to the GOP. Party activists—those who vote in primaries and volunteer to work for candidates—became more ideologically uniform within each party. In recent decades, party activists nominated candidates sharing the activists' ideological orientation. As these candidates gained election, the congressional GOP became more thoroughly conservative and the congressional Democrats more thoroughly liberal. Legislators' floor voting show a steadily increasing division between the parties. In recent years, this polarization has reached historically record levels, with the distance between the congressional parties in floor votes now greater than ever (Carroll et al. 2013). We explore congressional ideological divisions further in chapter 5. Now, a stable and unprecedentedly huge ideological divide characterizes the operations of the two major parties in Congress.

A growing ideological gap also appeared in the positions of the two parties' presidential candidates. The landmark years for this trend were 1964 and 1972. Barry Goldwater, the 1964 GOP presidential nominee, voiced a full-throated conservatism that reflected the takeover of the party's nomination process by activists of the political right. At the party's 1964 party convention, Goldwater's acceptance speech included a provocatively ideological claim: "Extremism in the defense of liberty is no vice" (Washingtonpost.com 2013). One of his supporters, Phyllis Schafly, wrote a pro-Goldwater book noting the great differences in the positions of the two 1964 presidential candidates—Goldwater and Democratic incumbent Lyndon Johnson—entitled *A Choice, Not an Echo* (Schafly 1964). Schlafy later became a leader of a conservative ideological group, the Eagle Forum. Another outspoken Goldwater supporter was the actor Ronald Reagan, who went on to win two terms as California's governor in 1966 and 1970. By the time of his election as president in 1980, the GOP was becoming more uniformly conservative and the ranks of moderate Republicans in state and national office were dwindling.

The ascent of a more emphatic liberalism in the Democratic Party began with the nomination of George McGovern as the party's presidential nominee in 1972. McGovern's candidacy encouraged the southern white exodus from the party to the GOP, reflected in McGovern's poor showing in southern states. His campaign adopted a series of then-controversial positions that now are mainstream positions for the Democratic Party. Those included support for abortion rights, ambitious environmental protection politics, reductions in military spending, and a less assertive foreign policy. Future Democratic president Bill Clinton worked for McGovern along with his spouse and subsequent Democratic presidential candidate Hillary Clinton. Barack Obama carries on the liberal tradition pioneered by McGovern. We explore the ideological presidency further in chapter 5. In recent decades, overall, Congressional officeholders and presidential aspirants became more consensual in their party's ideology and more distinct in their ideology from that of the rival party (Fiorina and Abrams 2009).

Contrasting ideological perspectives also shaped the public's voting since the 1960s. Political scientists William Claggett and Byron Shafer discovered that differences over social welfare policy have influenced much partisan voting over the last forty years (Claggett and Shafer 2010, 270). Ideology lies at the center of this division. Questions regarding who deserves welfare benefits, in what amounts, and whether the benefits should involve a work requirement have divided liberals from conservatives and Democrats from Republicans since the 1960s. From 1972 to 1988 in particular, the twin issues of public welfare and America's foreign policy shaped partisan voting. Democrats during this time disagreed with Republicans over the scale of defense spending and the use of the military overseas—again, major ideological divisions. With the end of the Cold War following the collapse of the Soviet Union in 1989, public welfare issues have remained important in partisan voting. Since then, another central divide shaping the public's partisan voting has concerned cultural issues regarding abortion, gay marriage, crime, gun control, and immigration (Claggett and Shafer 2010, 270–76). Democratic and Republican divisions on cultural issues, as reflected in recent party platforms, have been clear-cut. The major issues for the voting public have involved choices between two ideologically distinct parties.

Liberals, Conservatives, and Moderates Today

The patterns of ideological self-identification among the American public present a rich array of preferences varying by citizens' individual characteristics. Table 1.2 presents ideological self-identification by an array of personal characteristics. It reveals a nation very much divided by ideological labels. Men are 4 percent less liberal and more conservative than are women. Nonwhites identify as less conservative than do whites. Those of low income label themselves less conservative and more liberal than do those of higher incomes. The most liberal regions of the country are the Northeast and Pacific Coast, and the South and Mountain West rank as the most conservative regions. Midwest states lie between these two regional extremes.

Ideological leanings zigzag as peoples' years of education increase. The number of self-identified moderates declines as education rises. The "moderate" category is probably a resting place for those who do not think ideologically, a point we explore further in chapter 2. Those with postgraduate degrees are by far the most likely to identify as liberal or conservative. These two patterns are consistent with our earlier argument that higher levels of education produce more ideological thinking. High-school graduates, those with some college, and college graduates have the lowest levels of liberal iden-

TABLE 1.2
Demography of Ideological Self-Identification of Americans

	Percent Conservative	*Percent Moderate*	*Percent Liberal*
Men (46%)	37	38	25
Women (54%)	33	39	29
Whites (74%)	37	37	26
African Americans (15%)	24	47	29
Other races (12%)	34	38	28
Income under $25,000 (25%)	26	45	29
Income over $25,000 (75%)	35	37	28
South (37%)	39	40	22
Mountain West (8%)	39	35	26
Midwest (22%)	33	42	25
Northeast (17%)	31	34	35
Pacific West (16%)	29	38	34
Less than High School (16%)	29	44	27
High-School Degree (27%)	36	44	21
Some College (27%)	37	39	24
College Degree (16%)	39	35	26
Postgraduate Degree (14%)	28	28	44

Source: 2012 General Social Survey, National Opinion Research Center, University of Chicago.

tification and highest levels of conservative identification. The most liberal groups are those at the top and bottom of the educational scale—those with postgraduate degrees and those who have not finished high school.

Self-identification is a useful clue about ideological leanings, but the substance of one's ideology lies in a variety of attitudes about issues and situations. We explore the attitudes comprising citizens' ideology further in the next chapter.

Factions within American Liberalism and Conservatism

Given the partisan-ideological divisions among both the American public and its political leaders, one might assume that within the largely conservative GOP and liberal Democratic camps that uniformity of perspective reigns. In one sense that is true, in that many on each side of the divide share many issue opinions with their fellow partisans. In each camp, however, are interest groups attaching different priority to particular issues.

Among conservative Republicans, several factions are present. Social conservatives in organizations such as the National Right-to-Life Committee and National Association for Marriage place emphasis on cultural issues. National security conservatives such as the Committee on the Present Danger and Foreign Policy Initiative place top priority on military spending and an assertive foreign policy. Business groups such as National Federation of Independent Business (NFIB) and the Club for Growth focus on tax and regulatory issues. Libertarian groups such as the Republican Liberty Caucus seek smaller government in both domestic and military policy. The Tea Party, a grassroots movement originating in 2010 in response to President Obama's health care reform, is a far-flung conservative movement including all these three types of conservatives (Skocpol and Williamson 2012).

A wide range of differing issue priorities also exists among Democratic Party factions. Organized labor groups such as the American Federation of Labor–Congress of Industrial Organizations and National Education Association are concerned primarily with issues of workplace organization and union rights. Groups representing racial minorities, such as the National Association for the Advancement of Colored People (NAACP) for African Americans and the National Council of La Raza for Latinos emphasize issues such as affirmative action and racial discrimination. The Human Rights Campaign and National Gay Lesbian Task Force address gay marriage and sexual orientation issues. A large number of environmental groups, including the Sierra Club, Friends of the Earth, and Greenpeace focus on climate change and regulation of pollution. Progressive Democrats in organizations such as the Americans for Democratic Action press for lower levels of military spending.

As the national issue agenda expanded in recent decades, a wide variety of issue priorities emerged among interest groups allied with each of the major parties. That made coalition management a challenge for presidents and Congressional leaders as the various issue factions clamor for attention from elected officials. The varying priorities also create a vast range of ideological battles across the two parties. When particular issues arise, differing parts of each party's ideological coalition spring into action to challenge their partisan and ideological rivals. American politics probably now involves more arguments over more issues than ever before.

The Plan of the Book

In future chapters, we depict varying aspects of America's ideological politics. Chapter 2 explores ideology in the American public. Beyond the ideological self-identification discussed in this chapter, how extensive is ideological thinking among American citizens? Chapter 3 examines the geography of polarization. Some regions are predominately liberal—such as the Northeast and West Coast—while other sections—the South and Mountain West—are mainly conservative. We portray the historical origins and present consequences of these geographical divisions. Chapter 4 assesses ideology in Congress, including the record levels of partisan polarization in floor voting in both the U.S. House and Senate. Chapter 5 depicts the ideological presidency. Both George W. Bush and Barack Obama adopted ideological approaches during their presidencies and that requires explanation. Ideology in the federal courts is the focus of chapter 6. Since the 1960s, federal courts increasingly have engaged in policymaking, giving reign to ideological decision making. Chapter 7 charts America's ideological future. Our nation's politics is more ideological than ever before in our history. Is this America's new normal?

References

Associated Press. 2013. "House Republicans Hit Abortion, Immigration Hard, Saying GOP Elders Misinterpreted Romney's Loss." June 19. http://articles.washington post.com/2013-06-19/politics/40054253_1_house-republicans-abortion-republican-party (accessed June 26, 2013).

Brown, Brian. 2012. Brian Brown v. Dan Savage: The Transcript. August 26. http://johnshore.com/2012/08/26/brian-brown-vs-dan-savage-the-transcript/ (accessed June 26, 2013).

Carroll, Royce, Jeff Lewis, James Lo, Nolan McCarty, Keith Poole, and Howard Rosenthal. 2013. "D-NOMINATE Scores with Bootstrapped Standard Errors." February 17. http://voteview.com/dwnominate.asp (accessed June 27, 2013).

Claggett, William J. M., and Byron E. Shafer. 2013. *The American Public Mind: The Issue Structure of Mass Politics in the Postwar United States.* Cambridge: Cambridge University Press.

Danforth, John C. 2005. "Onward, Moderate Christian Soldiers." *New York Times.* June 17. http://www.nytimes.com/2005/06/17/opinion/17danforth.html (accessed June 26, 2013).

Edsall, Thomas B. 2013. "Now What, Liberalism?" *New York Times.* January 16. http://opinionator.blogs.nytimes.com/2013/01/16/now-what-liberalism/ (accessed June 26, 2013).

Eysenck, Hans J., and Glenn D. Wilson. (1978a). "Foreword." In H. Eysenck and G. Wilson, eds., *The Psychological Basis of Ideology.* Baltimore: University Park Press, vii–viii.

———. (1978b) "Conclusion: Ideology and the Study of Social Attitudes." In H. Eysenck and G. Wilson, eds., *The Psychological Basis of Ideology*, 303–12. Baltimore: University Park Press.

Ferguson, Niall. 2013. "The Regulated State of America." *Wall Street Journal.* June 18. http://online.wsj.com/article/SB10001424127887324021104578551291160259734.html (accessed June 26, 2013).

Fiorina, Morris C. 2013. "America's Missing Moderates: Hiding in Plain Sight." *The American Interest*. March/April. http://www.the-american-interest.com/article cfm?piece=1380 (accessed June 26, 2013).

Fiorina, Morris C., and Samuel J. Abrams. 2009. *Disconnect: The Breakdown of Representation in American Politics*. Norman: University of Oklahoma Press.

Flanigan, William H., and Nancy H. Zingale. 2010. *Political Behavior of the American Electorate*, 12th ed. Washington, DC: CQPress.

Foxnews.com. 2012. "Transcript of Romney's Speech at the RNC." August 30. http://www.foxnews.com/politics/2012/08/30/transcript-mitt-romney-speech-at-rnc/ (accessed June 26, 2013).

Gauchet, Marcel. 1996. "Right and Left." In P. Nora, ed., *Realms of Memory: Rethinking the French Past, Volume I—Conflicts and Divisions*, 241–300. New York: Columbia University Press.

General Social Survey. 1972–2012. National Opinion Research Center. University of Chicago. sda.berkeley.edu (accessed June 26, 2013).

Gerring, John. 1997. "Ideology: A Definitional Analysis." *Political Research Quarterly* 50 (4): 957–94.

Gibson, Ginger. 2013. "Boehner: More Energy Regs 'Absolutely Crazy.'" Politico.com. June 20. http://www.politico.com/story/2013/06/john-boehner-climate-change-obamacare-93110.html (accessed June 26, 2013).

Lowi, Theodore, Benjamin Ginsberg, Martin Shefter, and Stephen Ansolabehere. 2012. *American Government: Power and Purpose*. Core 12th ed. New York: Norton.

Marietta, Morgan. 2012. *A Citizen's Guide to American Ideology: Conservatism and Liberalism in Contemporary Politics*. New York: Routledge.

Merriamwebster.com. 2013 "Ideology." http://www.merriam-webster.com/diction ary/ideology (accessed June 26, 2013).

National Public Radio. 2012. "Affirmative Action: Is It Still Necessary?" February 27. http://www.npr.org/2012/02/27/147514069/affirmative-action-is-it-still-necessary (accessed June 26, 2013).

Newport, Frank. 2013a. "Republicans Put More Emphasis on Being No. 1 Militarily." February 27. http://www.gallup.com/poll/160727/republicans-put-emphasis-no-militarily.aspx (accessed June 26, 2013).

———. 2013b. "Nearly Half in U.S. Say Environmental Efforts Lacking." April 1. http://www.gallup.com/poll/161579/nearly-half-say-gov-environmental-efforts-lacking.aspx (accessed June 26, 2013).

Newsday.com. 2012. "Transcript of Paul Ryan's RNC Speech." August 29. http://www.newsday.com/elections/transcript-of-rep-paul-ryan-s-rnc-acceptance-speech-1.3937544 (accessed June 26, 2013).

New York Times. 2013a. "Obama's 2013 State of the Union Address." February 13. http://www.nytimes.com/2013/02/13/us/politics/obamas-2013-state-of-the-union-address.html?pagewanted=all&_r=0 (accessed June 26, 2013).

———. 2013b. "Transcript of Mitt Romney's Speech at CPAC." February 7. http://www.nytimes.com/2008/02/07/us/politics/08romney-transcript.html?pagewanted=all (accessed June 26, 2013).

Olson, Ted. 2010. "Text of Ted Olson's Opening Statement on Prop. 8—As Prepared." http://www.afer.org/press-releases/text-of-ted-olsons-opening-statement-in-prop-8-trial-as-prepared-2/ (accessed June 26, 2013).

Pew Forum on Religion and Public Life. 2013. "Changing Attitudes on Gay Marriage." June 10. http://features.pewforum.org/same-sex-marriage-attitudes/slide4.php (accessed June 26, 2013).

Pew Research Center for People and the Press. 2012. "As Fiscal Cliff Nears, Democrats Have Public Opinion on Their Side." December 13. http://www.people-press.org/2012/12/13/section-2-the-deficit-taxes-and-awareness-of-fiscal-cliff/ (accessed June 26, 2013).

———. 2013. "Broad Support for Renewed Background Checks, Skepticism about Its Chances." May 23. http://www.people-press.org/2013/05/23/broad-support-for-renewed-background-checks-bill-skepticism-about-its-chances/ (accessed June 26, 2013).

Schafly, Phyllis. 1964. *A Choice, Not an Echo: The Inside Story of How American Presidents Are Chosen.* Alton, IL: Pere Marquette Press.

Skocpol, Theda, and Vanessa Williamson. 2012. *The Tea Party and the Remaking of Republican Conservatism.* New York: Oxford University Press.

Torry, Jack, and Jessica Wehrman. 2013. "Brown Assails Obama's Budget: 'Senior Citizens Didn't Cause' the Recession." April 10. Columbus, Ohio *Dispatch.* http://www.dispatch.com/content/stories/local/2013/04/10/brown-assails-obamas-plan-to-reduce-senior-citizen-benefits.html (accessed June 26, 2013).

Washingtonpost.com. 2013. "Goldwater's 1964 Acceptance Speech." 1964. http://www.washingtonpost.com/wp-srv/politics/daily/may98/goldwaterspeech.htm (accessed June 26, 2013).

Whitehouse.gov. 2013a. "Remarks by the President at a DNC Event." June 12. http://www.whitehouse.gov/the-press-office/2013/06/12/remarks-president-dnc-event-miami-fl (accessed June 26, 2013).

———. 2013b. "Remarks by the President on the Affordable Care Act." May 10. http://www.whitehouse.gov/the-press-office/2013/05/10/remarks-president-affordable-care-act.

———. 2013c. "Remarks by the President at the Brandenburg Gate—Berlin, Germany." June 19. http://www.whitehouse.gov/the-press-office/2013/06/19/remarks-president-obama-brandenburg-gate-berlin-germany (accessed June 26, 2013).

Zelizer, Julian. 2013. "It's No Time to Retreat from Affirmative Action, Voting Rights." Cable News Network. June 10. http://www.cnn.com/2013/06/10/opinion/zelizer-court-race (accessed June 26, 2013).

2

Ideology in the American Public

I N OUR FIRST CHAPTER, WE DEFINED IDEOLOGY as a "set of fundamental beliefs or principles about politics and government: what the scope of government should be; how decisions should be made; what values should be pursued" (Flanigan and Zingale 2010, 135). We then reviewed the utility of ideology, considered ideology in the general American context, explored differences between liberals and conservatives, and briefly discussed the rise in partisan-ideological linkages in recent years. But important questions remain. For instance: Who defines a given ideology? How were the contours of contemporary liberalism and conservatism established? How do ideology and partisanship interact? Is there a top-down relationship between political elites and the people, where elites determine which policies constitute an ideology and the people adapt to follow that lead? Or is there a more democratic, bottom-up mechanism through which the people convey to elites the issues that are salient to them?

In chapter 1, we presented an overview of the dynamics of American liberalism and conservatism and discussed the increased ideological cohesion of the Democratic and Republican parties. In fact, many discussions of contemporary American politics treat ideology and partisanship as though they are synonymous. This is not very surprising given the clear evidence of both ideological and partisan polarization in Congress and in many state legislatures. There is clear evidence as well that the American electorate has sorted itself between the Democratic and Republican parties according to ideology (Abramowitz 2010). Indeed, it is quite common in media coverage of contemporary politics to see partisanship and ideology linked. Reporting on a bipartisan Senate deal that would extend unemployment compensation for several million Americans, the popular political news website Politico noted "Buy-in from progressive Democrats . . . illustrates a broad well of Democratic support for the bill, which lawmakers hope can prematurely quell any rebellion by liberals over concerns that too much was given to the GOP" (Everett 2014). Though the legislation was expected to receive majority support in the Democratic-controlled Senate, Politico noted a rougher sea in the Republican-controlled House of Representatives: "[T]he legislation still must go through a conservative House, where aides to Speaker John Boehner declined to offer an assessment of the Senate deal on Thursday" (Everett 2014).

It is an all-too-familiar scene in American politics, a battle of policy, dividing the two chambers of Congress and featuring a gulf between liberal Democrats and conservative Republicans. In such circumstances, who can bridge the divide? "Republican moderates could break this stalemate by threatening their own revolt," wrote Francis Barry of Bloomberg (Barry 2014). Moderates, however, appear to be in short supply. In February 2014, the *National Journal* referred to the 113th Congress as the most divided ever. "For the fourth straight year, no Senate Democrat was more conservative than a Senate Republican— and no Senate Republican was more liberal than a Senate Democrat. In the House, only two Democrats were more conservative than a Republican—and only two Republicans were more liberal than a Democrat" (Kraushaar 2014).

There is little dispute that the American Congress is populated by liberal Democrats, conservative Republicans, and a small group of moderates from both parties who stroll the wasteland between the two extremes. But what about the American electorate? Can we so easily assume that partisanship and ideology are as synonymous among the electorate? In some cases, especially among those most active in politics, the answer appears to be "yes." But move beyond that small group of political activists, or consider other periods in American history, and the relationship between partisanship and ideology becomes more complex. Though the two concepts may be related, they require separate consideration.

Ideology in America

Are Americans ideological voters? Do they make decisions on policy, party, and candidate support based upon a "set of fundamental beliefs or principles about politics and government: what the scope of government should be; how decisions should be made; what values should be pursued?" The most common approach to measuring ideology among the American public is via self-identification. In a typical survey, respondents are asked to identify themselves as liberal, conservative, or moderate. There is usually an option to allow a respondent to indicate that they either do not know or do not really care. Those who express no preference are usually asked which ideology they would choose if forced to pick. This approach to ideological classification is premised on two very important assumptions: (1) Most Americans are familiar with the concept of ideology and are knowledgeable as to the meaning of the liberal, conservative, or moderate classifications and (2) liberal, conservative, and moderate capture the full range of ideological thinking in America. As will be discussed later in this chapter, there is reason to believe neither assumption is correct. Most surveys allow for a seven-point ideology classification scale ranging from extremely liberal to extremely conservative, with moderate occupying the middle position. The seven-point scale is then condensed into a simple three-point scale (or a four-point, if "Don't Know" is included in the results).

The American National Election Studies (ANES) at the University of Michigan has been surveying the American electorate since 1948. Included among their battery of questions is one concerning ideology that has been asked in every survey since 1972. The results are presented in Figure 2.1. There

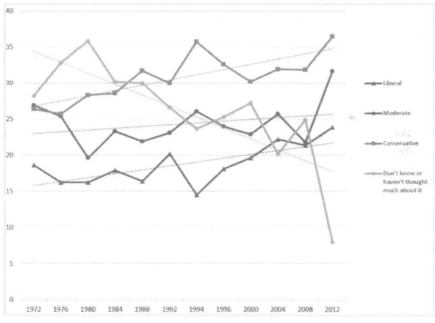

FIGURE 2.1
Ideological self-identification, 1972–2012.
Source: American National Election Studies.

are a few trends clearly evident in the data. The percentage of respondents self-identifying as either liberal or conservative has been rising since 1972. Conservative self-identification has increased from 26.4 percent in 1972 to 36.4 percent in 2012. Liberal identification has increased from 18.6 percent to 23.9 percent. The share of the population expressing no opinion or indicating a lack of thought regarding ideology has been declining—with a substantial drop in 2012. The share of moderates has been increasing as well, but the positive trend line is almost entirely driven by a jump in 2012. Between 1972 and 2008, there was a slightly negative trend in moderate self-identification.

Overall, the trend data presented in Figure 2.1 suggest a nation composed of an increasingly ideological public, though that assumption is premised on the notion that people know and understand what the ideological labels mean and are applying them correctly. It is certainly possible that many respondents hold beliefs and policy preferences that are inconsistent with their self-reported ideology. Additionally, the simple liberal, conservative, and moderate approach to classification largely precludes an understanding of ideology as a concept encompassing both social and economic policy dimensions. As discussed in chapter 1, contemporary American liberals occupy the liberal dimensions for both social and economic policy. Conservatives occupy both of the conservative dimensions. But libertarians and populists couple a liberal dimension with a conservative dimension. As a result, neither the liberal nor conservative classification would be appropriate and many may be identified as moderate or they may be identified with the ideology that corresponds to the dimension of greatest import to them.

The presence of the "don't know, haven't thought about it" options also cloud any assessment of the ideological composition of the American electorate. The manner in which we choose to deal with those who express no care or opinion can impact our assessment of the public. With the exception of 2012, the share of respondents expressing no ideology has hovered around 25 percent, or one-quarter of the electorate. Were we to simply drop them from consideration and focus solely on the remaining three categories, then the share of each would increase and we would conclude there are more ideological citizens than the data truly show. Table 2.1 reveals the impact of this seemingly simple choice based on 2008 survey data. If moderates and "don't knows" are considered collectively, then a clear plurality of voters, 46.3 percent, fall into the condensed category. Liberals and conservatives are dwarfed in comparison. However, if we decide that those who say they don't know or don't care cannot be easily classified and should be excluded from consideration, such a decision has a dramatic impact as well. Regardless of the approach taken, if assumptions about those with no preference are incorrect, then including them among self-identified moderates would yield a skewed picture of ideology in America.

TABLE 2.1
Alternate Measures of Self-Reported Ideology—2008

Self-Reported Ideology	Merging Moderate and "Don't Know"	Excluding "Don't Know"
Moderate	46.3%	29.0%
Liberal	21.8%	28.5%
Conservative	31.8%	42.4%

The traditional liberal or conservative approach to discussing ideology in America assumes a horizontal ideological spectrum with liberals at the left and conservatives on the right. Such an approach to explaining ideology assumes that Americans can be divided into two main camps: liberals, who favor economic intervention but oppose the promotion of traditional social values, and conservatives, who favor the promotion of traditional social values but oppose economic intervention. Economic intervention would include government policies such as progressive taxation, the redistribution of wealth, a safety net for the disadvantaged, or the regulation of business. Policies that promote traditional social values include restrictions on access to abortion and laws that define marriage as being between one man and one woman. Moderates supposedly occupy a position somewhere between the liberal and conservative camps near the middle of that horizontal spectrum. However, if we accept that there are social and economic policy dimensions to ideology, then we would expect the mix of policy preferences to allow for more than just conservatives, liberals, and moderates.

A sound approach to identifying the ideological preferences of the American electorate moves beyond simple self-reporting and placement along a left to right continuum. Claggett, Engle, and Shafer (2014) developed a set of policy *indicators* that capture voter positions on specific social and economic policy interventions. Based on these indicators, the authors developed a more complex picture of ideology in America that includes five ideological groups. In addition to liberals, conservatives, and moderates, the authors found a significant number of libertarians and populists. The combination of policy preferences held by each groups are presented in table 2.2.

Claggett and colleagues assigned survey respondents to the ideological classification that matched their stated policy preferences on an index of social welfare and cultural values questions. The authors then reviewed respondents' self-reported ideology on the traditional liberal, conservative, or moderate scale. They found that respondents identified as either liberal, conservative, or moderate based upon policy preference quite accurately self-described as either liberal, conservative, or moderate. Populists and libertarians, however, betrayed no preference for either policy dimension and

TABLE 2.2
American Ideological Classifications

Ideology	Policy Preference Economic Dimension	Policy Preference Social Dimension
Conservative	Opposes Economic Intervention	Supports Promotion of Social Values
Liberal	Supports Economic Intervention	Opposes Promotion of Social Values
Populist	Supports Economic Intervention	Supports Promotion of Social Values
Libertarian	Opposes Economic Intervention	Opposes Promotion of Social Values
Moderate	Essentially Occupies Center Ground on Both Dimensions	

Adapted from Claggett, Engle, and Shafer (2014).

self-identified as moderates; the implication of this finding being that the commonly used liberal, conservative, or moderate classifications overstate the share of moderates in the electorate. Claggett and colleagues do not offer a point in time estimate of the share of the electorate claimed by each ideological group, but do provide an average for the period 1992–2008.

As shown in table 2.3, the ideological breakdown based upon policy preference differs in important ways from the self-reported data in table 2.1. The share of liberals increases markedly when classification is based on policy preference and the share of moderates declines significantly when populist and libertarian options are included. The share of conservatives remains essentially unchanged. Though not shown, the share of liberals in the electorate has been increasing, while the share of libertarians and populists has declined. The shares of conservatives and moderates have remained relatively static. The partisan allegiances of these ideological groupings have changed over time and those shifting allegiances, coupled with the liberal/conservative parity, help to explain the partisan and ideological groupings that define contemporary American politics (Claggett, Engle, and Shafer 2014).

TABLE 2.3
Ideological Groupings Based on Policy Preference: 1992–2008

Ideological Grouping Based on Policy Preference	Share of the Electorate
Conservative	30.2%
Liberal	30.3%
Populist	10.5%
Libertarian	10%
Moderate	19.1%

Source: Claggett, Engle, and Shafer (2014).

Partisanship in America

In the simplest of terms, partisanship in the American context refers to one's political party affiliation. A person who consistently supports and votes for Democrats is a Democratic partisan, just as Republican partisans consist of voters who regularly support Republican candidates. Decades of research into the concept of partisanship demonstrates that it is so much more than that simple explanation suggests. Writing in 1960, Campbell et al. described partisanship as "a long-term, affective psychological attachment to a preferred political party" (Campbell et al. 1960). In their classic text, *The American Voter*, Campbell and colleagues likened the importance and influence of partisan identity to religious affiliation and social class. In short, partisanship defines someone. Partisanship is more than just voting for a Democrat or a Republican. Rather, it goes to the core of one's political beliefs or ideology.

Indeed, partisanship is a powerful influence. Research suggests that it determines how people react to the political world and respond to new issues. A growing body of research suggests that partisanship may be powerful enough to alter our perceptions of reality (Nyhan and Reifler 2010). In sum, partisanship acts as a filter that greatly influences how we see and interpret the world. Though that filter can be limiting in that it prejudices our judgment, it also saves time and effort and can facilitate political participation. A voter's partisan filter allows for an easier accommodation of new or controversial issues.

At the time of the 1972 Supreme Court decision legalizing abortion in *Roe v. Wade*, 410 U.S. 113 (1973), there was precious little difference between Republican and Democratic partisans regarding abortion. Over the course of the following decade, however, elites began to signal partisan positions on the issue. As party elites and opinion leaders increased their broadcasting of an "appropriate" partisan view on the issue, rank-and-file partisans began to fall in line. The debate over same-sex marriage offers another illustration. Opposition to same-sex marriage was once a bipartisan issue with majorities of Republicans and Democrats opposed. Following the 2004 presidential elections, Democratic Party elites began to express support for same-sex marriage. As the number of supportive elites grew, so too did support among Democratic partisans. Indeed, following President Obama's 2012 announcement that he too supported same-sex marriage, support among African Americans—a key Democratic Party constituency—jumped by nearly twenty percentage points (Clement and Somashekhar 2012).

Just as partisanship aids in the ability to absorb and respond to new and evolving issues, partisanship provides an electoral shorthand that allows voters to make choices in elections even when they know very little about the candidates. As discussed briefly in chapter 1, being a Democrat means something. The Democratic Party tends to support a more active federal government, a government that uses public policy to regulate business or protect the environment. Republicans tend to favor a limited government and prefer to allow the market to function as free from governmental interference as possible. Most Democrats favor abortion rights, while most Republicans oppose them. Most Republicans support limited gun-control measures and an expansive understanding of the Second Amendment's protection of the right to keep and bear arms, while most Democrats prefer more gun control and a limited interpretation of the amendment. Because of these party positions, voters are able to make reasonable assumptions about the policy beliefs of a candidate simply by knowing the candidate's partisan affiliation.

Those seeking office are aided as well by partisanship. Studies continue to show that partisans are fiercely loyal to their preferred party. In a typical presidential election, the Democratic candidate can expect to receive the support of roughly nine in ten self-described Democratic partisans and the Republican candidate can expect the same level of support from his or her fellow partisans. As a result, no major party candidate for office starts out with zero support. Rather, they have a base of support among their partisans in the electorate. Victory on Election Day results from building on that base.

Russell Dalton offers this summary regarding the importance of partisanship in American politics: "Partisanship is a central element in the functioning of citizens' political behavior. . . . Partisan ties: bind individuals to their . . . political party, . . . orient the individual to the complexities of politics; provide a framework for assimilating political information and understanding political issues; . . . guide in making political judgments; mobilize individuals to participate . . . ; provide a source of political stability" (Dalton 2013, 6).

So partisanship matters, but how partisan are Americans and how does partisanship relate to ideology? Though political scientists have been measuring public opinion and political attitudes for more than six decades, the question of Americans' partisanship is not an easy one to answer. The answer is clouded further by the growing tendency to conflate partisanship with ideology. It is at the intersection of partisanship and ideology that we find much of the debate regarding contemporary American politics, especially the discussion of ideological and partisan polarization.

Partisanship and Ideology in American Politics before 1964

When Campbell and colleagues undertook the first comprehensive study of partisanship for *The American Voter* in 1960, they determined that partisanship ran deep in America. As summarized by Russell Dalton, "[P]eople did not just vote for the Republican or the Democratic candidate, they considered themselves to be a Republican or Democrat" (Dalton 2013, 3). In 1964, roughly 93 percent of Americans self-identified as either a Democrat or a Republican. And the Democrats' 62 percent to 31 percent partisan-identification advantage closely imaged Democratic President Lyndon Johnson's 61 percent to 38.5 percent victory of Republican Barry Goldwater in the 1964 presidential election. Fewer than one in ten Americans described themselves as truly independent of party and only one in six indicated that they leaned more toward an independent status. Fully four in ten described themselves as strong partisans. As shown in Figure 2.2, the Democratic dominance of American politics began to unravel in the years after 1964. The story of the party's decline helps to illustrate important differences between partisanship and ideology. Prior to 1964, the Democratic and Republican parties were home to ideologically diverse coalitions. Both parties claimed a mix of economic and social liberals and conservatives, and partisanship was a powerful influence. In *The American Voter*, Campbell et al. described partisanship, or party identification, as an "unmoved mover." They argued party identification was sufficient to understand political attitudes and behavior, but attitudes and behavior were not sufficient to explain party identification. This was especially true in the case of ideology.

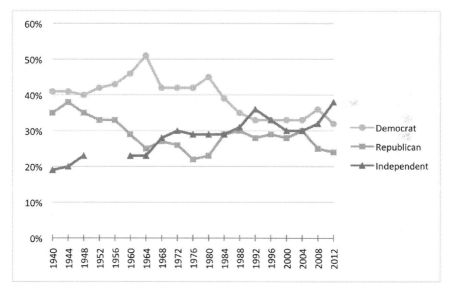

FIGURE 2.2
Changes in partisan identification, 1939–2012. Note: Data for Independents not available for 1952 and 1954.
Source: Pew Research Center for People and the Press.

As discussed in chapter 1, in contemporary American politics it would not be inappropriate to assume that an ideological liberal is a Democrat or that a Republican is an ideological conservative. In other words, in the current era partisanship helps explain attitudes and behaviors, just as attitudes and behaviors help explain partisanship. For a significant portion of the twentieth century, ideology and partisanship were poorly correlated. Yet political scientists at the time viewed partisanship as a lifelong attachment to party, an attachment that remained intact even when a partisan voted for candidates in another party.

This raises an interesting question: *If not ideology, then what motivated the partisan commitment?* To understand the partisanship dynamic in place at the time, consider another benefit of partisanship—it provides a sense of belonging. Members of a party are members of group and there are affective social benefits from group membership (Gerber et al. 2012). That's often why people join groups such as a fraternity or sorority or a college club or team. In addition to doing something they enjoy, they are expanding their social network and their source of support. Many political scientists challenge the unmoved mover understanding of partisanship. Indeed, they see partisanship as the end result of an individual's ongoing assessment and reassessment of the political world. As that world changes and new issues arise partisanship can change (or move) as well.

In 1964, political scientist Philip Converse, a coauthor of *The American Voter*, published *The Nature of Belief Systems in Mass Publics* in which he explored more deeply the issue of ideology and partisanship. Relying on ANES data from 1956 and 1960, Converse studied voter responses to a series of open-ended policy questions to determine whether respondents held "consistent" views across a range of issues. For example, a respondent expressing opposition to an expansive and growing welfare state would be expected as well to favor lower levels of taxation. Both positions are consistent with a conservative political ideology that prefers strict limits on the power and influence of government. Were the respondent to indicate support for the welfare state (a liberal view) while still favoring lower taxes (a conservative view) then such a response would indicate a lack of what Converse termed ideological *constraint*. Converse defined constraint as the degree to which a particular belief is predictive of another belief.

Several contemporary political issues illustrate ideological constraint. A candidate or voter who supports marriage equality for same-sex couples can be expected to support abortion rights, publicly financed health care, gun control, and government actions that limit greenhouse gas emissions. What's the connection between these seemingly unrelated policy positions? Each is consistent with contemporary liberal ideology. An individual's set of fundamental beliefs or principles constrains her issue positions. The absence of such constraint suggests the absence of any coherent or consistent ideology.

Converse found little evidence of ideological constraint among the American electorate at mid-century. In fact, he found evidence of true ideological constraint in fewer that 5 percent of voters. Nearly one in six voters seemingly lacked any real understanding of political issues or the policy preferences of the political parties—including their own party. Most voters, nearly half, made decisions regarding issues and candidates based on their favorable or unfavorable impact on social groups such as labor unions, business, farmers, or racial and ethnic minorities. Though these group-interest voters understood the policy issues that directly impacted their group, they demonstrated a lack of understanding of broader policy issues as well as party positions on those issues. Among this group, one might expect to find a union member who votes for Democrats, not because he is an ideological liberal but because he believes the Democrats to be the party of the working man. Approximately one in five voters based their decisions on the nature of the times and the party in or out of power. If Democrats were in power and the economy was weak, then one might expect these voters to hold Democrats to account and instead vote Republican. These voters lacked political sophistication and did not demonstrate any understanding of the broader policy positions of the parties. Single-issue voters, who are motivated to vote by support or opposition to a single policy issue, were counted among this group as well.

In all, Converse determined that fewer than 20 percent of voters demonstrated any discernable degree of ideological constraint. Among those who did, one tended to find better-educated Americans as well as political elites—those who discuss and are engaged in politics on a daily basis. Few Americans demonstrated a developed understanding of the policy positions of the two political parties, and absent an understanding of those positions, could not make decisions regarding personal partisanship based upon ideology. Converse concluded that Americans were not ideologues by nature.

Not all of Converse's contemporaries agreed with his conclusions. Some argued the apparent lack of sophistication among American voters was a reflection of poorly worded survey questions in the early years of the ANES. Subsequent reviews of ANES data collected in the 1970s suggested a greater degree of ideological constraint among the electorate. Again, some contended the evidence of greater constraint was actually a result of differently worded ANES questions. Beyond the possible influence of question construction, many researchers argue Converse's conclusions and categorization of voters are no longer relevant in a political world fundamentally different from the one he studied in the late 1950s and early 1960s.

Partisanship and Ideology in American Politics after 1964

Many political scientists agree the American political system underwent fundamental changes in the years following the 1964 presidential election (Aldrich and Niemi 1996; Schier and Eberly 2013). Following the Civil War and Reconstruction, the Republican Party was regarded as the party of civil rights and equality for African Americans. The party was strongest in the American Northeast (once a bastion of abolitionist sentiment) and in the Mountain West (states largely untainted by the nation's history of slavery). Democrats enjoyed their greatest strength in the states of the old, confederate South. Though Republicans had dominated much of national politics in the decades following the Civil War, that dominance waned considerably by the election of 1932 when Franklin Roosevelt and his fellow Democrats rode to political dominance on a tidal wave of public discontent.

However, students of contemporary American politics would be wrong to assume the partisanship, and especially partisan labels, conveyed the same information then as they do today. The Democratic Party that dominated American politics from the early 1930s through the mid-1960s was a party with a very diverse ideological coalition. Though the party was largely unified around the New Deal–era economic policies of Franklin Roosevelt—especially the creation of Social Security—there were significant differences in the area of social policy—especially in the area of racial equality. Northern Democrats favored expansive civil rights protections for African Americans and tended to vote for economic and social liberals. In the South, the majority white population supported economic liberalism but vehemently opposed the expansion of civil rights (Shickler 2013). The ideological division within the party is well captured by the fact that in 1964 the Democratic Party claimed the allegiance of 77 percent of African Americans (supporters of civil rights) and 71 percent of southern whites (opponents of civil rights) (Schier and Eberly 2013, 44). From 1952 through 1968, the party was composed of roughly equal numbers of liberals, conservatives, populists, and moderates and there were no real differences between the ideological makeup of party activists and rank and file party members (Claggett, Engle, and Shafer 2014). This diverse ideological coalition allowed the Democratic Party to dominate.

As detailed in table 1.1 in chapter 1, there is a multidimensionality to ideology. There are clear areas of economic liberalism and conservatism, such as tax policy or the regulation of business, and there is a social dimension evident in policy debates regarding abortion or same-sex marriage. For much of American history, politics was dominated by the economic dimension. In fact, party leaders and political elites worked to keep the social dimension out of politics as it presented a threat to party unity (Fiorina and Abrams 2009). The suppression of the social dimension was a key element of the Democrats' political ascension in the early 1930s as it allowed for a coalition of African American and southern white voters. Growing demands for federal civil rights guarantees and protections forced social policy to the fore of American politics and contributed to the current era of ideological/partisanship alignment.

The presidential election of 1964 offered voters a very clear choice between an economic and social liberal in incumbent Democratic president Lyndon Johnson and an economic and social conservative in Republican senator Barry Goldwater. Voters were offered a clear ideological choice in the 1964 election. They could vote for Johnson and endorse political liberalism or they could vote for Goldwater and embrace political conservatism. Although Lyndon Johnson won by a popular and electoral vote landslide, his victory came at the expense of the Democratic Party's diverse coalition and hastened the arrival of an era where partisanship and ideology became inextricably linked. Between 1972 and 1988, the share of liberals in the Democratic Party increased from one-fifth to one-third. The share of moderates and populists declined slightly, but the share of conservatives fell from one-quarter to less than one-fifth. Among Democratic Party activists the change was more dramatic. Among activists, the share of liberals increased from one-fifth to one-half and the share of populists and conservatives declined by half with each accounting for little more than one in ten Democratic activists (Claggett, Engle, and Shafer 2014). Very little changed within the Republican Party's ideological makeup between 1952 and 1988, with conservatives accounting for roughly 40 percent of party members.

In chapter 1, we defined American conservatism as a belief in "ordered liberty" best achieved in a culture that embraces tradition, personal responsibility, and restraint (Marietta 2012, 21). To most conservatives, an ambitious and activist government represents a threat to ordered liberty. American liberals, however, value the concepts of equality and justice more than they do liberty. To most liberals, government is viewed as a crucial partner in the promotion of social change often needed to realize the promise of equality and justice. A deference to tradition and restraint serves to protect the status quo. By the 1970s, the share of liberals within the Democratic Party was growing. Though conservatives had always composed the largest ideological bloc among Republicans, their numbers began to increase as well by the end of the 1980s. Between 1992 and 2008, ideological liberals grew to account for over 40 percent of rank-and-file party members and nearly two-thirds of party activists. Among Republicans, conservatives claimed just over 50 percent of rank-and-file members and two-thirds of activists. The Democratic Party became a more homogenously liberal political party and the Republican Party became homogenously conservative.

Alan Abramowitz (2010) demonstrated the high degree of homogeneity in the 2004 election and noted an increased correlation between partisan identification and ideology. According to Abramowitz, the big tent ideological coalitions of the Democratic and Republican parties, evident at mid-century, have been supplanted by ideologically homogenous parties. In Abramowitz's telling, the Democrats have become the partisan home of ideological liberals and the Republicans home to ideological conservatives. As a result of this ideological and partisan coupling, the American electorate has become quite polarized, with two political parties standing in stark opposition to one another. At the time of the 2004 election, Abramowitz determined that 56 percent of Democrats were ideological liberals and 73 percent of Republicans were ideological conservatives. Only 12 percent of Democrats were identified as ideological conservatives and 21 percent of Republicans were identified as ideological liberals. Relatively few partisans were identified as a moderates.

Contemporary American Politics and the
Intersection of Partisanship and Ideology

There can be little doubt that the Democratic and Republican parties are better sorted according to ideology and this sorting contributes to the tendency to conflate party and ideology in contemporary politics. But the question remains as to whether the American public has become more ideological and whether the public is more divided, or polarized, along ideological lines. Fiorina and Abrams (2009) contend there has been little increase in the degree of ideological thinking in America in the decades since Converse's initial study.

Are voters more ideologically polarized? The answer is a rather frustrating "yes" as well as "no." Figure 2.3 illustrates the difficulty in determining the correct answer. Consider the issue of abortion. Since the *Roe v. Wade* decision in 1972, the legality of abortion has been an ideologically polarizing issue in American politics. The following graph compares the attitudes of self-identified Democrats and Republicans regarding the legality of abortion in 1980 and in 2008. The light gray bar represents a liberal attitude (legal in all cases), the dark gray bar a conservative attitude (illegal in all cases), and the medium gray bar is a moderate position (legal in some cases). The data for 1980 reveal something interesting: in 1980, there was precious little difference between Democrats and Republicans regarding abortion. Roughly equal portions of each party opposed or supported abortion rights. But by 2008, we see a more familiar distribution of opinions. Democrats are now clearly the party of abortion rights and Republicans the party of abortion restriction. Members

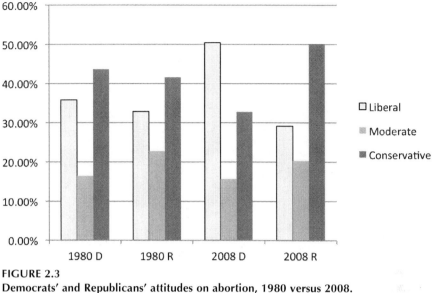

FIGURE 2.3
Democrats' and Republicans' attitudes on abortion, 1980 versus 2008.
Source: American National Election Studies.

of the two parties are polarized on the issue of abortion. So clearly we would expect our elected officials to mirror this mass polarization and refuse to compromise on abortion.

But does the abortion question actually reveal a polarized electorate? Does it truly demonstrate polarization at the mass level rather than the elite level? Figure 2.4 presents the same data presented in Figure 2.3, except for a single difference: instead of dividing the electorate into Democrats and Republicans, they are considered collectively (independent voters are excluded). What a difference that choice makes, and it illustrates the difference between polarization and party sorting. The data in Figure 2.4 make one thing very clear: the electorate is no more polarized today on the issue of abortion than it was in 1980, but the two parties are now deeply divided

So how do we explain the ideological polarization between identified Democrats and Republicans given little has changed when they are considered collectively? We explain it by looking to the actions taken by party activists to influence their party's national platform (Peters 2012). In 1972, liberal abortion-rights advocates pushed to have a plank added to the Democratic Party platform defending the legality of abortion, but the push failed. In 1976, party activists were able to insert the first supportive abortion language into the platform, but it was a mild statement: "*We fully recognize the religious and ethical nature of the concerns which many Americans have on the subject of*

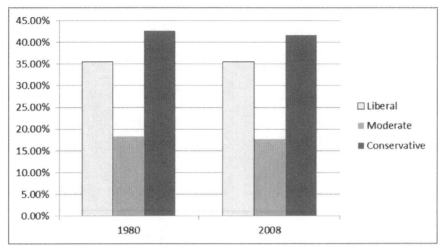

FIGURE 2.4
American attitudes on abortion, 1980 versus 2008.
Source: American National Election Studies.

abortion. We feel, however, that it is undesirable to attempt to amend the U.S. Constitution to overturn the Supreme Court decision in this area." In 1980, activists were able to expand the statement of support: *"We fully recognize the religious and ethical concerns which many Americans have about abortion. We also recognize the belief of many Americans that a woman has a right to choose whether and when to have a child. The Democratic Party supports the 1973 Supreme Court decision on abortion rights as the law of the land and opposes any constitutional amendment to restrict or overturn that decision."* Over time, the language became more bold, as in 1988: *"the fundamental right of reproductive choice should be guaranteed regardless of ability to pay"* and 2008: *"The Democratic Party strongly and unequivocally supports Roe v. Wade and a woman's right to choose a safe and legal abortion, regardless of ability to pay, and we oppose any and all efforts to weaken or undermine that right."*

Changes were taking place in the Republican platform as well. The party's 1976 platform barely mentioned abortion other than endorsing *"a position on abortion that values human life."* In 1980, conservative Republican activists made a more clear statement, while also recognizing differences of opinion: *"While we recognize differing views on this question among Americans in general—and in our own Party—we affirm our support of a constitutional amendment to restore protection of the right to life for unborn children. We also support the Congressional efforts to restrict the use of taxpayers' dollars for abortion."* By 2008, there could be no doubt regarding the Republican Party's position on abortion: *"We oppose using public revenues to promote or perform abortion. . . . We support the appointment of judges who respect traditional family values and the sanctity and dignity of innocent human life. We have made progress. The Supreme Court has upheld prohibitions against the barbaric practice of partial-birth abortion. States are now permitted to extend health-care coverage to children before birth. And the Born Alive Infants Protection Act has become law. . . . We must protect girls from exploitation and statutory rape through a parental notification requirement. . . . At its core, abortion is a fundamental assault on the sanctity of innocent human life."*

Over the course of three decades, party activists worked to define a Democratic and Republican Party position regarding abortion that suited their preferences. In more recent years, activists have worked as well to create clear divisions between the Republican and Democratic parties on issues such as same-sex marriage, the regulation of greenhouse gasses, and progressive taxation. Though these activists represent a small segment of the electorate and of each party, they exert tremendous influence over the direction of each party and therefore contemporary politics. These sharp party divisions have occurred even as the overall public has remained more moderate and accepting of compromise. Since the 1970s, there has been no decline in the share of Americans who describe themselves as moderate. During that same period, however, Americans believe the Republican Party is becoming more conservative and the Democratic Party more liberal (Fiorina and Abrams 2009). A recent national survey found that most Americans believe that a 50/50 compromise is the best outcome when Democrats and Republicans disagree on policy issues. Among ideological liberals and conservatives, however, only one-third supported the idea of equal compromise (Pew Research Center for the People and the Press 2014).

As liberals and conservatives sorted more neatly into the Democratic and Republican parties, populists, libertarians, and moderates were squeezed out. There is much discussion of the supposed rise of independent voters in contemporary politics and there is often a tendency to conflate independents and moderates. But the tendency to ignore libertarians and populists fosters a false impression of ideological homogeneity among independent voters In reality, independent voters include a diverse coalition of ideologies that no longer fit well with the two major parties.

Summary

Over the past several decades, liberal and conservative activists have worked to redefine the political parties in their ideological images. On a host of issue ranging from health care, taxation, welfare spending, abortion, and same-sex marriage, the parties are increasingly defined by their stark contrasts with one another. As the differences between the two parties became ever more clear, voters responded by more neatly sorting into the two camps. The overall electorate is no more divided by ideology today than it was thirty years ago, but the two political parties are much more divided and that division defines contemporary politics and discourse. Ideology and partisanship need not be synonymous, and for much of the twentieth century prior to the late 1960s, they were not. But today, it is understandable why many equate partisan Democrat with ideological liberal and partisan Republican with ideological conservative. And given that American politics is dominated by those two parties, the ideological sorting that has taken place translates into deeply divided political battles and creates the appearance of an increasingly ideological electorate. But when one considers the resultant displacement of populists, libertarians, and moderates as well as the marginal changes in the ideological distribution of the overall electorate, a more nuanced understanding of the intersection of partisanship and ideology emerges.

References

Abramowitz, A. 2010. *The Disappearing Center: Engaged Citizens, Polarization, and American Democracy.* New Haven, CT: Yale Press.

Aldrich, J., and R. Niemi. 1996. "The Sixth American Party System." In S. C. Craig, *Broken Contract: Changing Relationships Between Americans and Their Government,* 87–109. Boulder, CO: Westview Press.

Barry, F. 2014. *How Moderate Republicans Can Foil the Tea Party. Bloomburg.* March 14. http://politicsinminnesota.com/2014/03/francis-barry-how-moderate-republicans-can-foil-the-tea-party/ (accessed August 2, 2014).

Campbell, A., P. Converse, W. Miller, and D. Stokes. 1960. *The American Voter.* Chicago: University of Chicago Press.

Claggett, W., P. J. Engle, and B. Shafer. 2014. "The Evolution of Mass Ideologies in Modern American Politics." *The Forum* 12 (2): 223–56.

Clement, S., and S. Somashekhar. 2012. "After President Obama's Announcement, Opposition to Gay Marriage Hits Record Low." *Washington Post.* May 23. http://www.washingtonpost.com/politics/after-president-obamas-announcement-opposition-to-gay-marriage-hits-record-low/2012/05/22/gIQAlAYRjU_story.html?hpid=z3 (accessed August 2, 2014).

Dalton, R. 2013. *The Apartisan American.* Washington, DC: Sage.

Everett, B. 2014. "Jobless Deal Came Down to Wire." Politico. March 13. http://www.politico.com/story/2014/03/senate-unemployment-benefits-deal-104644.html#ixzz2vxxE9oO4 (accessed August 2, 2014).

Fiorina, M., and S. Abrams. 2009. *Disconnect: The Breakdown of Representation in American Politics.* Oklahoma City: University of Oklahoma Press.

Flanigan, W., and N. Zingale. 2010. *Political Behavior of the American Electorate.* Washington, DC: CQ Press.

Gerber, A., G. Huber, D. Doherty, and C. Dowling. 2012. "Personality and the Strength and Direction of Partisan Identification." *Political Behavior* 34:653–88.

Kraushaar, J. 2014. "The Most Divided Congress Ever, at Least Until Next Year." *National Journal.* February 6. http://www.nationaljournal.com/2013-vote-ratings/the-most-divided-congress-ever-at-least-until-next-year-20140206 (accessed August 2, 2014).

Nyhan, B., and J. Reifler. 2010. "When Corrections Fail: The Persistence of Political Misperceptions." *Political Behavior* 32 (2): 303–30.

Peters, G., ed. 2012. "Political Party Platforms of Parties Receiving Electoral Votes: 1840–2012." American Presidency Project. http://www.presidency.ucsb.edu/platforms.php (accessed September 15, 2014).

Schier, S., and T. Eberly. 2013. *American Government and Popular Discontent: Stability without Success.* New York: Routledge.

Shickler, E. 2013. "New Deal Liberalism and Racial Liberalism in the Mass Public, 1937–1968." *Perspectives on Politics* 11 (1): 75–98.

3

The Geography of Polarization

EVEN THE CASUAL OBSERVER OF AMERICAN POLITICS knows the 2000 and 2004 presidential elections yielded nearly identical regional patterns with regard to the states and Electoral Votes won by the Republican and Democratic candidates. Democrats were strongest in the so-called blue states of the Northeast and the Pacific Coast, while Republican strength was found in the "red" states of the South and the interior Midwest. In the years since, the notion of Red America battling Blue America has emerged as a major component of contemporary American politics. Though Barack Obama scored major victories in several traditionally red states in 2008, the striking visual of the Red/Blue divide continues to serve as evidence of an ever-deepening ideological divide in an America increasingly comprised of liberal Democratic and conservative Republican regions (Hopkins 2008). Commenting in September 2010, former President Jimmy Carter declared, "This country has become so polarized that it's almost astonishing. . . . President Obama suffers from the most polarized situation in Washington that we have ever seen even maybe than the time of Abraham Lincoln and the initiation of the war between the states" (Lubin 2010).

That is a powerful statement coming as it does from a former U.S. president. Even the most casual student of U.S. history would understand the gravity of the comparison. At the mid-point of President Barack Obama's first term, Carter was suggesting that the nation's first African American president faced a nation more divided than it was at the start of a bloody civil war; a war that divided the nation over issues of slavery and the rights of African Americans, both free and slave.

Could the United *States* of America be so divided? If so, what are the causes of the divide and how might researchers conceptualize or measure the division? Do states have their own culture? Is talk of deeply divided and polarized America just that—talk? Why do we care about states anyway?

A Nation of States

American government is built upon the concept of federalism. Merriam-Webster dictionary defines federalism *as the distribution of power in an organization (as a government) between a central authority and the constituent units (such as states)* (Merriam-Webster 2014). In the United States, the Constitution divides the power to govern between the one central, or federal, government and the individual states. Some governing powers are shared by each level, such as the power to levy taxes, while other powers are unique to one level, such as the federal government's power to issue currency. At the time of the Revolutionary War, the American colonies greatly differed from one another. They were settled at different times and for different reasons, and they had vastly different cultures and economies. In many respects, the individual colonies had greater ties to Britain than to each other. As a result, the nation's first constitution, the Articles of Confederation, created a confederacy of states with a very weak central government. After winning independence from Britain, the Articles of Confederation were replaced by a new constitution, the Constitution of the United States.

Many early leaders recognized the need for a more powerful central government. Under the Articles of Confederation, the individual states retained significant powers and the power of the central government was very limited. Though many acknowledged this was weakening the new nation, states were wary of surrendering their autonomy. Federalism was the solution to ease those concerns. The U.S. Constitution is replete with protections of and deference to state power and authority. Article I established a House of Representatives with members elected from each state and apportioned based on population. This compromise helped to secure the support of populous states. In the Senate, each state is granted equal representation in the form of two senators and Article Four guarantees the protection of state boundaries. Perhaps one of the most controversial and misunderstood examples of state deference is the Electoral College. The U.S. president is actually elected by the members of the Electoral College. On Election Day, voters go to the polls to vote for a slate of state electors committed to a specific candidate. The number of electors in a state is equal to the number of members in the House of Representatives plus the two senators. To win the presidency, a candidate must receive a majority of the votes cast by the Electoral College. This system makes the nationwide popular vote irrelevant in presidential elections. Rather, the election is a contest to win enough states to reach a majority in the Electoral College. In the case of a tie, or should no candidate receive a majority, the House of Representatives selects from the among the top three candidates—but each state gets only one vote regardless of the number of representatives in its delegation. Should the House fail to elect a president, then the vice president assumes the office. And who elects the vice president in the event of a tie or lack of majority? The Senate.

This side journey into U.S. political history and the role and power of states is not offered solely for the joy of the reader, rather it serves as a reminder that notions such as "states' rights," state sovereignty, and state culture are engrained deeply in the character of America. To state it more clearly, states matter in the United States. But studies of American politics and of ideology and partisanship often focus on the federal government and the overall U.S. population at the expense of state governments and populations. In recent years, however, greater attention has been paid to state politics. In the prior chapter, we explored briefly the debate over polarization in American politics and whether it was an elite-driven or mass-based phenomenon. Most early studies of polarization focused on national politics. In some respects, this was driven by the availability of data—whether it be congressional voting records or national opinion surveys. State-based data is not as readily available. To truly explore the issue of polarization and the impact of ideology on American politics states must be considered.

Identifying a State "Culture"

To many students of contemporary American politics, it may seem as though states can easily be classified into one of three groups, the red states that vote reliably for Republican candidates—especially at the presidential level—the blue states that vote for Democrats, and the swing states that tend to vary with regard to presidential preference. In truth, any attempt at political or cultural classification of states would be far more complex.

One of the best known attempts at identifying state cultures was Daniel Elazar's model of the moralistic, individualistic, and traditionalistic subcultures within the United States (Elazar 1966). Elazar defined political culture as "the particular pattern of orientation to political action in which each political system is embedded" (Elazar 1966, 78). To Elazar, political culture reflected the ethnic and religious values of the original settlers in specific regions of the country. As their descendants migrated west, they took their unique political cultures with them. To Elazar, a state's culture was central to understanding a state's ideology. Culture influenced ideology in three ways: (1) it influenced public perceptions regarding both the purposes of government and the extent of its power, (2) it established expectations for how much the public should be involved in influencing government and for which members of the public should have influence, and (3) it impacted the very practice of governing (transparent, corrupt, progressive, innovative, conservative) and the public's reaction to it. What Elazar described is very much what we present in this book as ideology.

Elazar argued there were three subcultures in America, with one dominant subculture evident in each state. Though a state's politics may be influenced by its dominant subculture, Elazar argued national politics results from the interaction of these subcultures, which he categorized as the individualistic, the moralistic, and the traditionalistic. In the individualistic political culture, government is designed to best serve the individual interests of those competing to influence and control the process. Innovation and the delivery of services are geared toward rewarding supporters and ensuring voter loyalty. Politics represents a means to an end and the ends often justify any means. Corruption and unethical behavior would be common and active public participation in government would be discouraged.

Standing in near stark contrast to the individualistic culture, Elazar defines a moralistic culture, which embraces collective action through politics, widespread civic engagements, and dedication to the needs of the community even at the expense of individual enrichments and private activity. The moralistic culture eschews corruption and the creation of policy simply to reward political supporters. Policy innovation is embraced, even if such innovations yield no electoral benefit. Finally, Elazar defines the traditionalistic culture as one concerned with the preservation of the status quo and social order. Government and politics is dominated by a small group of social elites based on their determinations of the public good and broad public participation is discouraged.

Elazar linked the culture of each state to the original colonists and their migration patterns. The moralistic states were mostly in New England and were settled by religious groups seeking freedom from persecution. These settlers wanted to create a society based on religious principles. The individualistic political culture originated in the states of the middle Atlantic that were settled by those seeking the opportunity to pursue individual success and wealth. The South was home to the original traditionalistic culture, a culture rooted in agriculture and built upon a foundation of slavery and controlled by a few landholding elites. As the descendants of the original settlers migrated westward, they took their culture with them. As a result, northern states are predominantly moralistic, southern states are traditionalistic, and states in between are individualistic.

As one may imagine, Elazar's theory of political culture is not without critics. One significant area of criticism being that the theory does not recognize or allow for the impact of regional migration. The United States has changed much since the days of the earliest settlers, and regional migration as well as waves of new immigrants from other nations undermines the notion of static political cultures. Criticisms notwithstanding, empirical analyses have shown that state political culture, as defined by Elazar, does correlate with factors such as political participation, policy innovation, and the generosity social welfare programs.

But the cultures identified by Elazar as less well correlated with issues such as partisanship and even ideology. The moralistic culture, with its focus on the community over the individual and belief in widespread civic participation, shares much with contemporary American liberalism. Yet a review of the moralistic states reveals conservative states such as Idaho, Kansas, and Utah alongside liberal states like California and Washington. The states sharing the individualist culture are incredibly diverse politically and include progressive states such as Massachusetts and conservative states such as Wyoming. Only the traditionalistic culture is home to a collection of states with conservative politics that share an emphasis on protecting the social order and the status quo.

It is worthy of note, however, that many of the moralistic states are aligned with more progressive politics, especially in national elections, and many of the individualistic states are home to very competitive state politics and are often considered to be swing states in national elections. This raises two interesting questions that will be explored in the remainder of this chapter: (1) can states truly be categorized as liberal or conservative and (2) does a state's political culture differ with regard to state and national politics? To answer both questions, we'll need to explore current research on state voting patterns in state and national elections and will delve into the contemporary debate regarding political polarization in the United States. Whereas Elazar saw regional groupings of states sharing a dominant culture brought by original settlers, many contemporary researchers see state political cultures being formed or fortified by Americans choosing to "vote with their feet" and relocate to live among kindred ideological spirits.

Political Division in the American States: A Big Sort?

Talk of political divisions between states is quite common in discussions of contemporary American politics. Conservative icon and radio talk show host Rush Limbaugh refers to the American West Coast as the *Left Coast* in an effort to poke fun at the liberal ideological reputation of California and Washington State. Contributors to the liberal website Daily Kos often describe the swath of states from Nevada to Georgia—states routinely won by conservatives—as "jesusland." Certainly talk of divided states is not new to American political discourse. The nation did, after all, fight a bloody civil war based largely on differences between northern and southern states regarding slavery and the power of the federal government to address the issue. Years after the end of the U.S. Civil War, tensions between the North and the South lingered. During the American civil rights era in the 1950s and 1960s, it was often northern liberal politicians engaged in battle with southern conservatives. And yet, for a time, there remained a rather collegial relationship between northern and southern politicians despite seemingly clear ideological differences regarding civil rights.

The collegial relationship between northern and southern states during the civil rights era likely reflected the simple fact that states from both regions were members of the same diverse political coalition—the Democratic Party. Beginning with the election of 1932, the Democratic Party dominated American politics and the party routinely laid claim to both southern and northern states. Republican strength was found in the states of the Midwest. The geographic divisions that define contemporary American politics still tend to be regional—North, South, West, Midwest, and Mountain West—but now the divisions are partisan as well as ideological. The partisan differences between states appears to be introducing a level of animosity and antagonism in politics that was absent for much of the twentieth century.

Perhaps the first hints of the new partisan and ideological division between states emerged in the election of 1964 between Democrat Lyndon Johnson and Republican Barry Goldwater. Though Johnson was a southerner, with a long political career in Texas, his embrace of civil rights for African Americans placed a tremendous strain on his relationship with conservative southern states. Though Johnson won a resounding victory, Goldwater was victorious in the line of states in the deep South from Louisiana to South Carolina. Throughout the south the Republican received greater support than any prior Republicans. Unlike Democrats in prior elections, Johnson found his greatest support in the North. In spite of Goldwater's loss, 1964 proved to be a pivotal election as it marked the beginning of a political realignment in which the base of Republican support shifted to the South and Democratic support shifted north (Schier and Eberly 2013). The shifting of the electoral landscape was not immediate, but electoral coalitions steadily emerged providing reliable and predictable support for the two parties.

The emergence of reliably Republican and reliably Democratic states did not go unnoticed by political scientists. The razor-thin Electoral College victories secured by George W. Bush in 2000 and 2004 resulted in the creation of the now commonplace Republican Red State v. Democratic Blue State maps. The supposed stability of the electoral map was bolstered by the fact that only two states (Iowa and New Mexico) switched party columns in the 2004 election as compared to 2000. A review conducted just prior to the 2008 election determined that twenty states were reliably Republican and nineteen (including the District of Columbia) reliably Democratic (Pollard 2008). States were defined as reliable if they voted with their respective party's candidate in at least four of the five elections between 1988 through 2004. Between 1988 and 2004, Republicans were strongest in the South, the Great Plains, and the Mountain West, while Democrats tended to be strongest in the Northeast, Great Lakes, and on the West Coast. Twelve swing states—Arkansas, Florida, Iowa, Kentucky, Louisiana, Missouri, Nevada, New Hampshire, New Mexico, Ohio, Tennessee, and West Virginia—were not consistently in either party's column during that time frame. In 2008, Barack Obama won all nineteen of the reliably Democratic states, but he also carried six of the twelve swing states, and claimed four previously reliable Republican states—Colorado, Indiana, North Carolina, and Virginia.

In 2012, Barack Obama repeated his 2008 electoral success, surrendering only Indiana and North Carolina. But Obama's margins were diminished in Colorado and Virginia as well as in the six swing states that he carried. Obama's largest margins were secured in the nineteen reliably Democratic states, and Republican Mitt Romney secured his largest victory margins in reliably Republican states as well as Arkansas, Kentucky, Tennessee, and West Virginia. Though the election between Obama and Romney was a relatively close 51 to 47 percent race, in many states the two candidates were separated by landslide proportions of 20 percentage points or more. Obama won five states plus the District of Columbia and Romney eleven states by margins exceeding twenty percentage points.

At the county level, the landslide victory margins were even greater. But these state and local landslides were not new to the 2012 election. Political researchers had noted over the course of recent elections that such lopsided election results were becoming the norm in American presidential politics. It was as if the nation was experiencing what political scientist Bill Bishop (2009) called the Big Sort. Bishop examined county-level presidential election results for each election between 1976 and 2008 and the trend he discovered is quite suggestive. In 1976, approximately 26 percent of Americans lived in counties won by one presidential candidate by a landslide margin of at least twenty percentage points. In 1992, the number had risen to 38 percent living in a landslide county, by 2004 the share was at 50 percent, and in 2008 it was at 75 percent.

Based on the trend he discovered, Bishop concluded "most places, most communities in the nation, are growing more politically one-sided—either more solidly Democratic in presidential elections or more reliably Republican. The 'red' and 'blue' maps of the states are totally misleading. The real differences in American politics today are found at the level of the community. We're increasingly sorting into communities that reliably vote Democratic or Republican in presidential elections" (Bishop 2008). Bishop notes that many factors appear to contribute to Americans opting to vote with their feet and move to new communities, including education and job opportunities. Bishop does not argue that people are making a conscious decision to move to communities populated by people with similar ideologies. Instead, he sees the sorting as a by-product of the fact that partisan affiliation is strongly related to underlying attitudes, views, and beliefs (ideologies) that influence people's perceptions of the world and of their surroundings. In other words, there is a correlation between ideology and many lifestyle preferences such as community amenities. Given the increasingly strong relationship between ideology and party affiliation discussed in chapter 2, it is reasonable to conclude that ideology may indirectly influence where people choose to live. As a result, Americans may be sorting into ideologically homogenized communities—landslide communities—and creating geographic polarization.

Recent changes at the state level appear to support Bishop's big sort theory. Prior to the 2008 election, Arkansas, Kentucky, Louisiana, Tennessee, and West Virginia were considered to be swing states as none had been consistently won by either party between 1988 and 2004. Since 2000, however, each of these states have voted Republican and Arkansas, Kentucky, Tennessee, and West Virginia surpassed the twenty-point landslide threshold in 2012 and now appear to be safe Republican states (Schier and Eberly 2013). Though Barack Obama won the 2012 election by a narrow 51 percent to 47 percent margin, the margin between Obama and Romney exceeded twenty percentage points in eighteen states and Washington, D.C., and the margin exceeded fifteen percentage points in nine other states. The elections of 2000, 2004, and 2012 were each decided by margins of less than four percentage points. The closeness of those results fuel discussion of a divided nation, even as presidential candidates are winning by landslides at the state level. Only four states were decided by a margin of less than four percentage points in 2012—suggesting a divided nation comprised of very lopsided states.

Figure 3.1 divides the country into strong and competitive Republican and Democratic states. Strong states include those in which the Democratic or Republican vote share averaged 54 percent or more during the 2000, 2004, 2008, and 2012 elections. Competitive states averaged between 50 and 53.9 percent. Pure toss-ups were limited to states in which neither party averaged at least

Moralistic	Individualistic	Traditionalistic
California	Connecticut	Alabama
Colorado	Delaware	Arizona
Idaho	Illinois	Arkansas
Iowa	Indiana	Florida
Kansas	Nebraska	Georgia
Maine	Nevada	Kentucky
Michigan	Maryland	Louisiana
Minnesota	Massachusetts	Mississippi
Montana	Missouri	New Mexico
New Hampshire	New Jersey	North Carolina
North Dakota	New York	Oklahoma
Oregon	Ohio	South Carolina
South Dakota	Pennsylvania	Tennessee
Utah	Rhode Island	Texas
Vermont	Wyoming	Virginia
Washington		West Virginia
Wisconsin		

FIGURE 3.1
Daniel Elazar's state political cultures. Source: Elazar (1966).
Note: Alaska and Hawaii were not included.

50 percent of the vote. The states are sorted based on relative strength of partisan vote. When averaged across the 2000 to 2012 election cycles, thirty-four states plus the District of Columbia emerge as either strong Republican or strong Democratic states. Only four states stand out as pure toss-ups at the presidential level.

Political scientist Alan Abramowitz describes the electoral divide demonstrated in table 3.1 as one of "geographic polarization" (Abramowitz 2010, 118). As noted by Abramowitz, there has been a rather consistent pattern of geographic polarization in presidential elections since 2000. Even Obama's comfortable election margin in 2008 did not break from the pattern of numerous landslide states and relatively few closely divided states. Such geographic polarization represents a departure from past elections when landslide states were the exception and not the rule. The elections of 1960 and 1976 were quite close nationally and there were very few landslide states. Only three states and Washington, D.C., were decided by margins exceeding twenty points in 1976 and only four states in 1960. Some of the tightest state contests were waged in the most populous states like California, New York, and Texas. California and New York are now landslide states for Democrats and Texas is nearly a landslide state for Republicans.

Abramowitz and Bishop see a nation steadily sorting into Democratic (liberal) and Republican (conservative) strongholds—strongholds that endure even when a candidate from an opposing party scores a decisive national victory. Barack Obama carried twenty-eight states in 2008 and he won twenty-one of them by margins exceeding ten points and by a margin of less than five points in only four. Though Senator John McCain lost the race by a seven-point margin and secured only 173 electoral votes in twenty-two states, he won fifteen of those states by margins exceeding ten points and by a margin less than five points in only two. The apparent lack of competitiveness in so many states, even in the face of closely fought races, has been described as "one of the most striking changes in American elections over the past four decades" (Abramowitz 2010, 714).

What are the implications of this geographic sorting? Bishop contends that there are positive aspects of having states that seemingly embrace a particular party or ideology. National politics in America is marked by stalemate and gridlock as control of government either vacillates between short periods of control by a single party or control is divided between two parties with deep ideological differences. States that are free from divided government and that have stable single-party control are better able to engage in policy experimentation. As discussed earlier in this chapter, American federalism allows for tremendous state autonomy in policymaking and policy experimentation. Geographic sorting would enable safely Democratic states to explore progressive policy solutions to problems such as global climate change or the delivery of health care services. Republican states could experiment with free-market approaches to education reform such as vouchers for private schools. National, state, and local policymakers could observe these experiments and make decisions based on what was or was not successful. Were all states as narrowly divided and gridlocked as the national government, there would be little opportunity for experimentation and observation.

But there are downsides to geographic polarization as well. American democracy was premised on the notion of diverse perspectives being brought together in a system of checks and balances that force compromise. In Federalist 10, James Madison famously warned against the dangers of faction, and by faction Madison meant a group such as a political party organized around a common set of beliefs or objectives, such as an ideology. Madison warned of the dangers to liberty posed by unchecked factions as they pursue their objectives with little to no concern for the rights and concerns of others. The American system of government was designed to minimize the potentially harmful effect of factions. Under the U.S. system, factions were to be forced to recognize and work with other factions in pursuit of a common interest reached through compromise. Representatives were elected from among the populace in such a way that no single faction was likely to dominate. Madison advocated a broad field of play that would encompass multiple perspectives.

The smaller the society, the fewer probably will be the distinct parties and interests composing it; the fewer the distinct parties and interests, the more frequently will a majority be found of the same party; and the smaller the number of individuals composing a majority, and the smaller the compass within which they are placed, the more easily will they concert and execute their plans of oppression. Extend the sphere, and you take in a greater variety of parties and interests; you make it less probable that a majority of the whole will have a common motive to invade the rights of other citizens. (Federalist 10)

Madison feared the prospect of single-faction dominance. He believed that representative government would decrease its likelihood. In many respects, geographic sorting and polarization represent Madison's fears come to life. If political scientists such as Bishop and Abramowitz are correct about geographic sorting and polarization, then in many states and localities a single faction, the Democratic or the Republican Party, has taken hold. In such circumstances the interests of the party are pursued at the expense of compromise and inclusiveness. Keep in mind, even in a state where Barack Obama won by a 60 to 40 percent margin, there is still a sizable share of the electorate that did not vote for him. Though the 60 percent majority may be in a position to govern without compromise or consideration of the 40 percent, such an approach to governance is contrary to the American ideal.

If states and counties are becoming more ideologically homogenous, then those elected to represent the states or congressional and state legislative districts will likely reflect the ideological preference of the majority. In the so-called landslide areas, there would be little need for elected officials to consider, let alone represent, the interests of the minority. The more ideologically homogenous states and counties and representative districts become, the greater the likelihood that our legislative bodies such as the U.S. Congress or state legislature will be populated by members representing two ideologically homogenous parties. In the absence of true ideological or electoral competition at home, these members will have little incentive to seek out common ground and compromise with the opposition party. As stated by Bishop,

> The Founders sought to make diversity a creative force. Differences didn't have to end in hate. They could be wielded to craft the best answer to problems. The Founders sought to turn the vice of disagreement into the virtue of new understanding. Now that simply doesn't happen—in Congress, in our legislatures, or between our increasingly isolated neighborhoods. We've replaced a belief in a nation with an oversized trust in ourselves and our carefully chosen surroundings. (Bishop 2008)

Bishop warns the sorting of Americans by ideology creates geographic echo chambers. Increasingly, voters find themselves in communities, congressional districts, and even states where a single party, linked to a coherent and consistent ideology, dominates political discourse. In such areas, there is little opportunity to engage with those who may have a different perspective.

Rather, the tenets of the dominant ideology are continuously reaffirmed and emphasized. In such circumstances, opposing viewpoints are often dismissed or ignored with little to no consideration. This fosters ideological extremism and intolerance of those with differing opinions, the end result being a deeply divided citizenry, polarized political parties, and unproductive or nonexistent political discourse (Cho, Gimple, and Hui 2013).

It is important to note there is evidence of geographical ideological sorting beyond that of just presidential election results. Abramowitz has compared voters in Republican red states with their counterparts in Democratic blue states and determined they have different priorities for and expectations of government—likely reflecting important ideological differences. According to Abramowitz, red state voters tend to be more religious, are more likely to own a firearm, are more likely to be prolife with regard to abortion, and are more likely to oppose marriage equality for same-sex couples (Abramowitz 2010).

The evidence of a deeply divided and regionally polarized America is compelling, but does it really prove the existence of a Red/Blue divide? Do lopsided results in presidential elections truly indicate geographic polarization at least partially driven by ideology? Many political scientists disagree with Bishop's big sort theory and the notion of ideologically driven geographic sorting and polarization. To these critics, the evidence of an ideological awakening followed by a regional sorting has been overstated and proponents of the theory overlook considerable contrary evidence.

Political Division in American States: A Big Exaggeration?

A chief critique of the regional ideological sorting argument is its reliance on presidential election results as the key indicator. As argued by Morris Fiorina, votes cast represent choices made by voters, but those choices cannot be used as evidence of a voter's position on specific issues (Fiorina and Abrams 2009). The distinction between making a choice in a particular election and taking a position on a specific policy issue is crucial when considering ideology. Remember, an ideology is a set of fundamental beliefs or principles about politics and government. Though it may seem reasonable to assume that a vote cast for a presidential candidate is indicative of a voter embracing that candidate's beliefs and principles or policy positions, there is truly no way to know that with any degree of certainty. Additionally, making such an assumption requires an additional assumption that voters are fully informed and aware of a candidate's beliefs, principles, and positions.

Fiorina argues that the rise of landslide counties and states may be a reflection of candidate ideology and not state, county, or voter ideology. In 1976, for example, voters were asked to choose Jimmy Carter, a conservative southern Democrat, or Gerald Ford, a moderate Midwestern Republican. In 2004, voters were asked to choose John Kerry, a liberal New England Democrat, or George W. Bush, a conservative southern Republican. Given the growing ideological distance between candidates since the 1970s, it's understandable how states and counties may vote overwhelming for one candidate over the other, even if state or voter ideologies have not changed (Fiorina and Abrams 2009).

Another limitation of the reliance on presidential election results is the focus on a single national election. If ideology captures a foundational set of beliefs, then one would expect to find evidence of ideology not just in a single presidential vote, but in votes for Congress, and state and local elections as well. And presidential elections may be a poor choice to serve as a proxy for a voter's underlying beliefs. Since the early 1970s, presidential candidates for the two major parties have been selected via a nomination system that relies heavily upon primaries, caucuses, and state party conventions. Participation and turnout for this nominating process tends to be low and dominated by ideologically motivated voters. As a result, presidential candidates often reflect the preferences of the ideological bases of the competing parties. In America, that means conservative Republicans pick the Republican nominee and liberal Democrats pick the Democratic nominee. In recent years, the Democratic and Republican candidates have used polarized rhetoric to heighten the sense of urgency and importance in selecting one party over the other (Schier and Eberly 2013). The same process is typically employed by states for the nomination of Senate and House races. If the two selected candidates are ideologically polarized, then voters are compelled to make a seemingly polarized choice on Election Day, though that choice may belie a preference for less ideologically rigid candidates. Elections are typically very good at telling us who won, but very bad at telling us why they won.

If presidential elections do result from primaries that produce polarized candidates and election strategies that use polarizing rhetoric to motivate voters, then looking to other elections may be worthwhile. If ideology is so important to Americans that it is contributing to a great national sort and creating lopsided, monolithic, landslide states and counties, then surely the evidence of such ideological motivation is evident in measures other than the presidential vote shares.

In a series of articles, Robert Erikson, Gerald Wright, and John McIver used state-level survey data to measure changes in within state ideology over time (Wright, Erikson, and McIver 1985, 1987) (Erikson, Wright, and McIver 1993) (Wright et al. 2000). The authors determined there was very little evidence of intrastate ideological change between 1976 and 1998, a time period when Bishop and Abramowitz contend that geographic sorting was under way. Paul Brace and colleagues built on existing research into state-level ideology by constructing a state-by-state dataset that combined findings from the American National Election Studies with the General Social Survey. The researchers were able to study ideology in thirty-five states from 1974 through 1998 and found no evidence of ideological change during that time in twenty-eight of the thirty-five states (Brace et al. 2004). Only three states were found to demonstrate ideological change by both the Brace et al. and Erikson et al. studies: California, Oregon, and West Virginia. Thomas Carsey and Jeffrey Harden examined partisanship and ideology in states in 2000, 2004, and 2006, and found little evidence of ideological shifts during that time period. In fact, the authors found a tremendous amount of ideological and partisanship overlap across states (Carsey and Harden 2010).

Stephen Ansolabehere and colleagues (2006) explored average overall vote margin, average presidential vote margin, and measures of "safe states" and unified state governments and determined states are quite competitive arenas for partisan politics. The study even found that the South is the most politically diverse region in the country, contrary to the popular idea that it is a bastion of the national Republican Party. Eric McGhee and Daniel Krimm (2009) studied voter-registration data within states and determined there has been a large and pervasive increase in registered independents in recent years and little evidence of ideological or partisan polarization. The authors argued that estimates of state ideological polarization based on presidential vote share are misleading as voters have no alternative choice to the two candidates. Given our discussion of five ideological groupings found in America, the lack of an alternative choice in most elections means populists, libertarians, and moderates choose between a Democratic (liberal) and Republican (conservative) candidate. As such, equating their choice with their ideology would be quite misleading.

A recent study by Sam Abrams (2011) examined presidential, senatorial, and gubernatorial elections during the 1992–2008 time frame, the period during which Bishop argues the big sort took place. Much like Bishop, Abrams confirmed the pattern of few landslide counties in 1992 rising steadily until 2008 where the majority of counties were landslide counties. If voters are motivated by ideology and the two parties are well defined by two competing ideologies, then one might expect senatorial and gubernatorial races to follow the same pattern as presidential races. This is not the case. Abrams found that landslide senatorial elections have been common and more likely than presidential landslides since at least 1992 and have held steady. With regard to gubernatorial elections, there appear to be no clear patterns. Landslide counties were more prevalent before 2000 and reveal a very inconsistent pattern in the years since. If Americans were sorting by ideology and ideology was a driving force in American politics, it would be reasonable to assume that the trend lines for landslide counties would be roughly the same for presidential, senatorial, and gubernatorial elections. This is not the case.

Next, Abrams considered the consistency of voting. He compared the share of counties in which one party won the presidential contest in each of the five elections between 1992 and 2008; he called these "solidly partisan" counties. Next, he considered those counties in which one party won four of the five elections and the counties in which one party won two or three of the five elections. He labeled these counties "leaning partisan" and "moderate," respectively. His findings at the presidential level appear to support the emergence of ideologically sorted landslide counties as nearly 60 percent were found to be solidly partisan. Approximately 15 percent were in the leaning partisan category and slightly more than 30 percent were classified as moderate. Abrams then added gubernatorial and senatorial elections to the mix to consider voting consistency during the 1992–2009 time frame. The results were quite different. Fewer than 30 percent of all counties voted for the same party in gubernatorial and Senate elections from 1992 to 2008. Roughly one-third of counties were determined to be leaning partisan and just less than one-third were deemed to be moderate. Perhaps more surprising, when Abrams divided his election comparison into two time periods, 1992–1999 and 2000–2009, he found that the share of polarized counties was smaller in the more recent time period—polarization in counties is not more common now than in the 1990s, it is less common.

The list of strong and competitive states in presidential elections presented in table 3.1 also highlights the limitation of relying on the presidential vote to estimate polarization or state ideology. As of summer 2014, ten of the strong or competitive states had divided party control of state government and four had unified party control—but not under the party that consistently wins presidential elections. Prior to the 2014 elections, there were thirty-seven states with unified party control of state government. That number fell to thirty after the election. The number of states with divided party control of state legislatures increased from three to eight after the 2014 midterms. Additionally, three of the strongest Democratic states in presidential elections, Illinois, Maryland, and Massachusetts, elected Republican governors in 2014. Partisan control of legislative chambers flipped in ten states (National Council of State Legislatures 2014). It is hard to reconcile Abrams findings with arguments that Americans are sorting by ideology and are more divided than at any time since the Civil War.

Ian McDonald (2009) studied the question of voter migration and the increase in landslide counties to see if there was a connection between district growth and partisanship. McDonald theorized that if people are voting with

TABLE 3.1
Strong and Competitive Republican and Democratic States—2000–2012

Strong Republican	Competitive Republican	Pure Toss-up	Competitive Democrat	Strong Democrat
Utah	Missouri	Ohio	Michigan	D.C.
Wyoming	North Carolina	Florida	Oregon	Hawaii
Idaho	Arizona	Colorado	Pennsylvania	Rhode Island
Oklahoma		Virginia	New Mexico	New York
Nebraska			Wisconsin	Massachusetts
Alabama			Minnesota	Vermont
Kansas			Iowa	Maryland
North Dakota			New Hampshire	Connecticut
Alaska			Nevada	California
Kentucky				Delaware
Texas				Illinois
South Dakota				New Jersey
Mississippi				Maine
West Virginia				Washington
Louisiana				
Arkansas				
Tennessee				
South Carolina				
Montana				
Indiana				
Georgia				

their feet and seeking ideologically compatible communities, then one might expect to see increased partisanship or polarization in the fastest-growing districts in the country. After examining congressional district growth and change during the 1990s and the 2000s, McDonald found no evidence of partisan sorting taking place. There were no discernable differences between districts that were experiencing growth (a proxy for voter in-migration) and of districts that experienced no growth. Though some showed partisan sorting, others showed partisan convergence (the parties neared parity) or dilution (a dominant party was weakened). But sorting, convergence, and dilution happened across growing and static districts in a manner that suggested no pattern or relationship.

The lack of any discernable sorting would come as little surprise to Samuel Abrams. In addition to his research on landslide counties, Abrams explored the extent to which Americans feel connected to their communities. If people are moving to areas better suited to their underlying values and beliefs, then it stands to reason that they would be aware of the preferences of those around them. Abrams found that most Americans describe their relationship with their neighborhood, town, or city as not very close or not close at all. Reviewing findings from a 2008 Pew Foundation poll, Abrams notes as well that fewer than 12 percent of respondents indicated being "Very Involved" in neighborhood or community activities. Nearly half indicated little to no involvement. The study revealed as well that nearly two-thirds of Americans indicate knowing 25 percent or fewer of their neighbors, and of the neighbors they know, they speak with less than half on a regular basis. When neighbors do talk, they rarely discuss politics and respondents indicated being unaware of the political leanings of roughly 25 percent of the neighbors with whom they interact. Abrams found little to support the notion of a sorting public.

A central tenet of the big sort theory holds that voters are making a conscious and informed decision to move to areas more in line with their preferences. It is important to note that Bill Bishop, the author of *The Big Sort*, does not contend voters are relocating to areas with like-minded voters as the result of a conscious decision to seek out communities of individuals with similar ideologies or partisan preferences. Rather, Bishop argues that people choose communities based on a host of personal preferences—preferences for community structure, open spaces, or close-knit walking communities, churches, or museums—and such preferences are correlated with ideological views. As a result, Bishop contends Americans are inadvertently sorting into politically like-minded communities. So the extent to which voters discuss politics or interact with their neighbors may be of little relevance to sorting.

A 2014 study by the Pew Research Center (2014) offered support for Bishop and for Abrams. The study, "Political Polarization in the American Public," explored the impact of ideology on many aspects of public life. A key set of questions asked respondents what they cared most about in their communities and social circles. As shown in Figure 3.2, greater than three-quarters of ideological liberals expressed a clear preferences for communities with smaller homes positioned close to one another where schools and other amenities where within walking distance. At the other end of the ideological spectrum, three-quarters of ideological conservatives preferred larger houses spaced farther apart with schools and other amenities located miles away. Ideological liberals expressed a clear preference for living in a city or urban setting while ideological conservatives expressed a preference for a rural or small-town existence. Such a clear difference in community preference, along ideological lines, could contribute to ideological sorting but the Pew study also found that only one-fifth of the public could be categorized as either consistently liberal or consistently conservative.

The Pew study found as well that most Americans share a general agreement regarding what matters most in a community. As shown in Figure 3.3, regardless of ideology, overwhelming majorities want to live near family, in

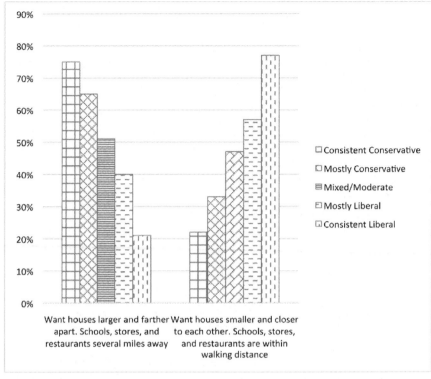

FIGURE 3.2
Community preferences by ideology.
Source: Pew Research Center for the People and the Press.

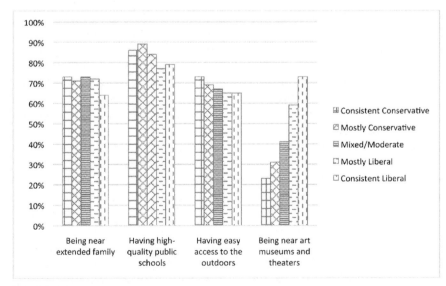

FIGURE 3.3
What matters most in a community by ideology.
Source: Pew Research Center for the People and the Press.

areas with quality schools, and have easy access to outdoor activities. Perhaps the only area ideological divided concerning community amenity preferences was the importance of being near a museum.

The Pew study found little indication of respondents caring whether family members married someone with opposing political viewpoints, who owned a firearm, was of a different race, or who came from outside the United States. Though ideological liberals and conservatives discussed politics more often than others, only one-third of ideological liberals and one-half of ideological conservatives expressed a preference to live in a community of like-minded people. The Pew study did find that the share of consistent liberals and consistent conservatives increased by 11 percentage points over a twenty-year period, but that only resulted in an increase from 10 percent in 1994 to 21 percent in 2014. So ideologues have doubled in size over a twenty-year period, but they are only one-fifth of the electorate.

A Big Sort or a Big Shrug?

Is America dividing along ideological lines? It's difficult to say. Though there is a clear indication that many regions, states, and counties have become reliably partisan in presidential elections, there is equally clear evidence that those regions are much less reliably partisan in nonpresidential elections. There is evidence as well that the most ideological voters tend to have few friends outside of their political party and disapprove of family members marrying outside of their political party. But most Americans appear to care little about the beliefs of those who family members marry, or of their friends' political beliefs. Do Americans want to live near people who share their beliefs? Again, with the exception of approximately one-half of the small group of ideological conservatives and one-third of the equally small share of ideological liberals the vast majority of everyone else does not appear to care (Pew Research Center for the People and the Press 2014).

While books such as *The Big Sort* and Abramowitz's *The Disappearing Center* contend ideological thinking and political polarization—especially at the county and community level—has been on the rise during the past few decades, there is reason to question those conclusions. A substantial body of research reveals little support for the notion of a mass electorate sorting along ideological lines. Contrary to the theory that lopsided presidential election results indicate increased ideological alignment within states and counties, multiple studies have concluded there is little evidence of ideological change taking place within states. The landslide county argument is challenged as well by research showing senatorial and gubernatorial elections do not follow the same pattern and there remains considerable political competition within states. Additionally, recent research suggests that American ideology is far more complex than a simple liberal, conservative, and moderate divide. Though liberals and conservatives may dominate American politics and America's main political parties, there remain a significant number of populists and libertarians that do not fit well into any "Big Sort" theories (Claggett, Engle, and Shafer 2014).

References

Abramowitz, A. 2010. *The Disappearing Center: Engaged Citizens, Polarization, and American Democracy.* New Haven, CT: Yale University Press.

Abramowitz, A. 2013. The Electoral Roots of America's Dysfunctional Government. *Presidential Studies Quarterly, 43*(4), 709–31.

Abrams, S. (2011). In Search of the Big Sort. *Southern Political Science Association Annual Meeting.* New Orleans.

Ansolabehere, S., R. Jonathan, & J. Snyder Jr., 2006. Purple America. *Journal of Economic Perspectives, 20,* 97–108.

Bishop, B. 2008. *Big Sort Maps.* Retrieved from The Big Sort: http://www.thebigsort.com/maps.php.

Bishop, B. 2009. *The Big Sort: Why the Clustering of Like-Minded America Is Tearing Us Apart.* Boston: Mariner Books.

Brace, P., K. Arceneaux, M. Johnston, & S. Ulbig, 2004. Does State Political Ideology Change over Time? *Political Research Quarterly, 57*(4), 529–40.

Carsey, T., & J. Harden, 2010. New Measures of Partisanship, Ideology, and Policy Mood in the American States. *State Politics & Policy Quarterly, 10*(2), 136–56.

Cho, W. T., J. Gimple, & I. Hui, 2013. Voter Migration and the Geographic Sorting of the American Electorate. *Annals of the Association of American Geographers, 103*(4), 856–70.

Claggett, W., P. J. Engle, & B. Shafer, 2014. The Evolution of Mass Ideologies in Modern American Politics. *The Forum, 12*(2), 223–56.

Elazar, D. J. (1966). *American Federalism: A View from the States.* New York: Crowell Company.

Erikson, R., G. Wright, & J. McIver, 1993. *Statehouse Democracy: Public Opinion and Policy in the American States.* Cambridge, MA: Cambridge University Press.

Fiorina, M., & S. Abrams, 2009. *Disconnect: The Breakdown of Representation in American Politics.* Oklahoma City: University of Oklahoma Press .

Hopkins, D. 2008. The Rebirth of Regionalism: Geographic Polarization in Federal and State Elections. *American Political Science Association Annual Meeting.* Boston.

Lubin, G. 2010. *Jimmy Carter Says US Is More Polarized Now Than During Civil War.* Retrieved August 14, 2014, from Business Insider: http://www.businessinsider.com/jimmy-carter-says-us-is-more-polarized-than-during-civil-war-2010-9.

McDonald, I. 2009. Polarization in High-Growth U.S. House Districts. *American Political Science Association Annual Conference.* Toronto.

McGhee, E., & D. Krim, 2009. Party Registration and the Geography of Party Polarization. *Polity, 41*(3), 345–67.

Merriam-Webster. 2014. *Federalism.* Retrieved August 10, 2014, from Merriam-Webster Dictionary: http://www.merriam-webster.com/dictionary/federalism.

National Council of State Legislatures. 2014, November 6. *StateVote 2014: Election Results.* Retrieved November 14, 2014, from National Council of State Legislatures: http://www.ncsl.org/research/elections-and-campaigns/statevote-2014-post-election-analysis635508614.aspx.

Pew Research Center for the People & the Press. 2014. *Political Polarization in the American Public.* Retrieved June 13, 2014, from http://www.people-press.org/2014/06/12/political-polarization-in-the-american-public/.

Pollard, K. 2008. *Swing, Bellwether, and Red and Blue States: Demographics and the 2008 U.S. Presidential Election.* Retrieved August 11, 2014, from Population Research Bureau: http://www.prb.org/Publications/Articles/2008/electiondemographics.aspx.

Schier, S., & T. Eberly, 2013. *American Government and Popular Discontent: Stability without Success.* New York: Routledge.

Wright, G., R. Erikson, & J. McIver, 1985. Measuring State Partisanship and Ideology with Survey Data. *Journal of Politics, 47,* 469–89.

Wright, G., R. Erikson, & J. McIver, 1987. Public Opinion and Policy Liberalism in the American States. *American Journal of Political Science, 47,* 980–1001.

Wright, G., J. McIver, R. Erikson, & S. Holian, 2000. Stability and Change in State Electorates: Carter Through Reagan. *Annual Meeting of the Midwest Political Science Association.* Chicago.

4

The Ideological Presidency

No political leader in the United States—and probably the world— receives more public and media attention than does the president of the United States. Why? Because of America's leading role in the world and the president's position as its sole chief executive who, according to the Constitution, must ensure that the laws are "faithfully executed." A president's policy positions and performance in office has a big effect on the role of ideology in U.S. politics. To the extent that a president thinks and acts ideologically, America's national politics become more ideological.

The many roles played by chief executives create large presidential effects on how citizens think about issues concerning ideological categories of liberalism and conservatism. Political scientist Clinton Rossiter identified several roles played by modern presidents (Rossiter 2012). Constitutionally, the president is commander in chief of the armed forces. The president's "commander" role involves him in many issues of national security about which conservatives and liberals disagree. George W. Bush's initiation of the Iraq war in 2003 spawned much liberal dissent. Conservatives derided Barack Obama's conduct of the war in Afghanistan and initial withdrawal of troops from Iraq as insufficiently resolute. A related presidential role is as an international leader of our allied nations. Global issues of terrorism, economic growth and inequality, and the environment involve the chief executive in matters about which great ideological divisions exist between conservatives and liberals in the public and in government.

Constitutionally, the president also performs the role of chief executive, in charge of implementation of a wide range of national policies. Ideological disputes regularly accompany the president's execution of policy. George W. Bush encountered Democratic and liberal opposition to his implementation of "faith-based" social services. Barack Obama's implementation of the Affordable Care Act, his health care reform, faced implacable conservative and Republican opposition. Rivals of both chief executives accused them of staffing the executive branch with ideologically extreme appointees.

In addition, the president operates as leader of his party. Party leadership involves the president in ideological disputes with partisan rivals. Both George W. Bush and Barack Obama frequently took to the stump to decry the wrongheaded priorities of rival partisans. The related role of leader of Congress in recent years has proven to be a strongly partisan and ideological duty of presidents. In our Congress chapter, we noted how the House and Senate are strongly polarized by partisan and ideological differences. In response, recent presidents have actively taken sides in partisan and ideological legislative disputes, producing party-line support and opposition for the initiatives of both George W. Bush and Barack Obama.

When attempting to perform the role of leader of public opinion, presidents regularly advocate for a particular set of ideological positions. George W. Bush frequently argued for the conservative goal of limited government: "My concern about the role of the federal government is that an intrusive government, a government that says, 'don't worry, we will solve your problems' is a government that tends to crowd compassion out of the marketplace" (Mitchell 2000). Barack Obama trumpeted liberal principles when advocating greater economic equality: "This growing inequality, it's not just morally wrong, it's bad economics. When wealth concentrates at the very top, it can inflate unstable bubbles that threaten the economy. When the rungs on the ladder of opportunity grow farther and farther apart, it undermines the very essence of America, that idea that if you work hard, you can make it here" (Shear and Baker 2013).

In recent decades, presidents have augmented their impact by claiming new unilateral powers. Unilateral means actions accomplished by the president through his sole initiative and direction. These include executive orders, executive agreements, presidential memoranda and proclamations, and reorganization plans. Executive orders have the force of law unless canceled by majority votes in the House and Senate or annulled by a later president. Executive agreements are diplomatic accords between the United States and other nations of limited scope that do not need ratification by the Senate by a two-thirds majority, as do broader scale international treaties. Presidential proclamations and memoranda announce policy changes or specific ways to implement policies. They resemble executive orders but usually involve smaller-scale initiatives. These constitute a handy toolkit for chief executives as they make their mark on policy and government. They are an efficient means for a president to impose his ideological vision on aspects of national politics and policy.

George W. Bush's conservative approach to embryonic stem-cell research appeared early in his presidency in a 2001 executive order. The order limited federal funding for such research, which had drawn objections from orthodox religious leaders. It sparked much dissent from liberals, who viewed them as dangerous threats to scientific progress (Seelye 2001). Barack Obama's executive order in 2013 delaying implementation of his health care reform for one year enraged conservative opponents of the reform who argued that the president had no such power in the law to suspend its implementation. Obama delayed implementation in order to lessen difficulties with the initiation of the law, but ideological opponents of the law wanted it completely repealed (Dorning and Wayne 2013).

The above examples come from the George W. Bush and Obama presidencies because these chief executives governed in an ideological fashion, heightening the ideological conflicts in American politics. We can trace the rise of the modern ideological presidency back to the arrival of Ronald Reagan in the White House in 1981, as we note later in this chapter. First, it is necessary to examine the two factors that shape the degree to which a presidency is ideological. Those are (1) the presidential selection process and (2) how presidents use their powers once in office. If the presidential selection process yields strongly ideological nominees, the winner likely will operate as an ideological president. Does the presidential selection process produce more ideological nominees and presidents?

Ideology in Presidential Nominations

Recent presidents have been more ideological than their predecessors because the process that selected them advantages those with strong ideological views. The presidential selection process is a prime venue for ideological activism. Its very structure advantages those with strong motivations. Those with relatively extreme policy views, as we noted in previous chapters, engage in more political activities than do those with moderate views.

The crucial first stage of presidential selection is the nomination of presidential candidates by the two major parties. The nomination process is participatory—that is, it advantages those most motivated toward political activism. It involves delegate selection in fifty separate states beginning in Iowa in February of a presidential election year and concluding in several states in June, before the late summer nominating conventions.

Most states use a primary system for selecting national convention delegates. On primary election day, those so motivated turn out and vote to select delegates for the candidate of their choice. In practice, only a small minority of partisans in a state—10 to 20 percent—bother to vote in a primary election. A minority of states uses a caucus/convention process for selecting delegates. This is a multistage affair occurring over several months, beginning with caucuses in every precinct of the state. Caucus meetings take several hours and select delegates to county or state legislative district conventions, who then select a smaller set of delegates to congressional district and state conventions, where they choose national convention delegates. The caucuses that start the process feature much smaller turnouts—2 to 3 percent of the state's partisans—than do primary elections.

So it falls to that minority of partisans motivated enough to spend time in the primary polling booth or at a caucus meeting to determine each major party's presidential nominee. The activists in presidential caucuses and primaries are often ideologically extreme and unrepresentative of the broader population of partisans in their states (Nivola 2005). As political scientist Morris Fiorina puts it, political parties and presidential nominations are dominated by "coalitions of minorities who seek to impose their views on the broader public" (Fiorina and Abrams 2009, 98). To paraphrase Woody Allen, so much in life depends on showing up, and the strongly ideological show up in dominant numbers in presidential caucuses and primaries, producing liberal Democratic and conservative Republican presidential nominees. That has been the case in the United States, particularly since 2000.

Table 4.1 presents evidence of increasing ideological extremism in presidential nominations. It charts public perceptions of presidential nominees' ideological positions and the self-described ideological positions of party activists. On a one-through-seven ideological self-identification scale, with one most liberal and seven most conservative, the public since 1972 has placed itself just slightly right of center, a bit greater than four, the moderate category in the scale. Active and very active partisans—defined in terms of the number of different political activities in which they engaged—were somewhat distant from the average ideological identities of voters. Active and very active Republicans labeled themselves conservatives, just less than six on the scale. Active and very active Democrats labeled themselves liberals, close to two on the scale. The very active partisans in just about every year since 1972 were ideologically more extreme—further from the public average—than were less active partisans.

Also evident in table 4.1 is the distance between the public's perceptions of each major party nominee's ideological position since 1972. For Democrats, the biggest deviations from the public average occurred in 1972, when

TABLE 4.1

Public Perceptions of Presidential Nominees' Ideological Positions and Partisans' Self-Described Ideological Positions 1972–2012

Year	Average Public Score	Diff Dem Nominee	Diff R Nominee	Diff Active Dems	Diff Active Rs	Diff Very Active Ds	Diff Very Active Rs
1972	4.14	-1.69	0.73	-1.73	1.33	-1.81	1.41
1976	4.23	-0.98	0.67	-1.85	1.36	-2.12	1.33
1980	4.31	-0.57	0.9	-1.89	1.32	-2.02	1.58
1984	4.24	-0.79	0.72	-1.88	1.41	-2.1	1.38
1988	4.37	-1.13	0.74	-1.99	1.29	-2.26	1.3
1992	4.21	-1.02	0.83	-1.86	1.4	-2.03	1.38
1996	4.35	-1.13	0.7	-1.99	1.38	-1.99	1.63
2000	4.28	-1.04	0.66	-1.87	1.48	-1.94	1.58
2004	4.23	-1.24	0.89	-1.87	1.54	-2.07	1.75
2008	4.24	-1.28	0.74	-2.04	1.51	-2.28	1.56

Source: American National Election Studies.

Democrats nominated the strongly liberal George McGovern, and since 2004. The public ranked recent nominees John Kerry in 2004 and Barack Obama in 2008 and 2012 as more liberal than previous nominees, reflecting the enhanced impact of ideological liberalism in the Democratic Party's nomination process. GOP nominees rate as more conservative than the public average but closer to that average in most years than the Democratic nominee. Only Ronald Reagan in 1980 rated further from the public's average ideology than his Democratic rival, incumbent Jimmy Carter.

Examples of emphatic liberalism and conservatism appear in each of the parties' 2012 platforms, embraced by their party's nominees. The Democratic platform endorsed the Affordable Care Act—Obama's major expansion of the federal government's role in health care—advocated a higher minimum wage, legal abortion, gay marriage, action on climate change, ending the Afghan war, and cooperation with Russia. The contrasting GOP platform called for repeal of the Affordable Care Act, a balanced federal budget, banning legal abortions, defense of traditional marriage, higher defense spending, resolve in the Afghan war, a tougher policy toward Russia, and domestic energy independence.

The composite picture emerging from table 4.1 and the 2012 party platforms is one of two parties dominated by ideological activists who nominate presidential candidates reflecting their ideology. The evidence is consistent with a view that parties insist "on the nomination of candidates with a demonstrated commitment to its program and works to elect those candidates to office. . . . Parties mainly push their agendas and aim to get the voters to go along" (Bawm et al. 2012, 571–72).

Ideological Voting in Presidential Elections

Ideology is a central concern of party activists and presidential candidates. It occupies a less central but important role in the decisions of recent presidential election voters. Political scientist William Jacoby found that in both 2000 and 2004, "there was widespread recognition of the candidates' and parties' ideological positions" and that "individuals' evaluations of those stimuli were shaped by their personal liberal-conservative orientation" (Jacoby 2009, 584, 591). In those elections, however, ideology did not directly affect voters' presidential choices. Instead, it operated indirectly through other more direct influences—perceptions of candidates' personalities, policy issue attitudes, and economic judgments—to affect the vote choice. A person's ideology shaped judgments about personalities, policies, and the economy and those more specific attitudes directly stimulated vote choice.

In 2008, however, Jacoby found ideology playing a more direct role in voters' choices, with liberalism promoting a Democratic vote and conservatism a GOP vote. "This effect is uniform throughout the electorate with no appreciable tendency for the impact of ideology to increase along with a person's level of political sophistication. The result shows that ideology was an important force in determining the choices of American voters during the 2008 election" (Jacoby 2010, 562). Ideology now not only directly shapes the behavior of presidential candidates and party activists, but of the voters themselves.

Ideology has a new centrality for voters because of an unprecedented level of ideological polarization that shapes party affiliations in the twenty-first century. In recent decades, ideological thinking has become more widespread among the politically active and more partisan citizens. It now affects a broader range of their political behaviors. The result is "an increasing connection between individuals' expressed partisanship and their self-reported ideology and a stronger connection between both partisanship and expressed liberal-conservative ideology and the opinions of Americans on policy-related issues" (Bafumi and Shapiro 2009, 18). Partisans increasingly link their personal ideological label—liberal or conservative—to their policy opinions and partisan affiliations. That makes Democrats more liberal and Republicans more conservative.

Among active citizens, the party–policy–ideology links are thus stronger. That has produced, particularly in presidential elections since 2000, emphatically liberal Democratic platforms and candidates and emphatically conservative GOP platforms and candidates. Does this pattern translate into presidential governance? Does the public perceive recent presidents as clearly ideological figures as they govern the nation?

Ideology and the Public Presidency

Once elected to the White House, the president is the most conspicuous American citizen. Every action and statement receives careful scrutiny by the White House press corps, and any notable presidential statement or action spreads throughout the nation and world via the Internet, radio, and television. It would follow that if political activists, presidential candidates, and even voters use ideology to guide their actions, the public would tend to identify a president by his ideology.

Over his time in office, more citizens become able to evaluate an incumbent president. In surveys, they register additional specific "likes" and "dislikes" about an incumbent and are better able to register how "warm" or "cool" about the president on a "feeling thermometer" ranging from zero to one hundred degrees (Burden and Hillygus 2009, 624–25). As time passes, public opinion about presidents also polarizes around partisan affiliation, with partisans of the president's party and those of the rival party differing in their approval. This partisan divergence has swollen into a great gap during the presidencies of George W. Bush and Barack Obama. Two reasons account for this increase: "both a long-term increase in the polarization of partisan evaluations of candidates and a short-term jump in polarization that comes as part of any president spending time in office" (Burden and Hillygus 2009, 630).

The "approval gap" for recent presidents Obama and George W. Bush reached the highest levels ever recorded in the seventy years of Gallup polls. The "gap" measured the average job approval for a president among both Democrats and Republicans. Obama's average approval gap during his first term was 76 percent, with 86 percent of Democrats approving but only 10 percent of Republicans. During George W. Bush's first term, 91 percent of Republicans approved but only 15 percent of Democrats did. The approval gap has a distinctly ideological dimension and identical gap of 76 percent (Jones 2013). Since 1972, a related "ideology gap" has grown for presidents. It is the average distance in perceived presidential ideology among a president's partisans and rival partisans in the public. That gap—on the seven-point liberal–conservative ideology scale—has doubled since 1972, increasing from one to two points (Newman and Siegel 2010, 354). The public's partisan and ideological polarizations regarding presidents go hand-in-hand.

The Partisan Presidency

Recent presidents contributed to this increased partisan and ideological polarization in the way they have conducted themselves in office. Political scientist Richard Skinner identified the traits of the current "partisan presidency" which is a presidency with a strong ideological profile. The originator of this new mode of presidential governance was the emphatically conservative Ronald Reagan, who took office in 1981. Table 4.2 lists its characteristics. They contrast with those of the "modern presidency" created by Franklin Roosevelt in the 1930s and existing through the presidency of Reagan's predecessor, Jimmy Carter.

Presidents no longer gain support across party lines, as incumbents Dwight Eisenhower and John F. Kennedy did in the 1950s and 1960s. Partisan presidents instead reinforce the polarization by favoring friendly media sources such as Fox News, talk radio (for conservatives), or MSNBC (for liberals) rather than focusing only on inclusive messages for the overall public as they

TABLE 4.2
The "Modern Presidency" and the "Partisan Presidency"

Subject	"Modern Presidency"	"Partisan Presidency"
Congressional Relations	President's party often divided; work across party lines	Partisan polarization: president works closely with own party, has difficult relations with opposition
Executive Administration	Rely on nonpartisan experts, civil servants; patronage in decline	"Administrative presidency" for partisan/ideological ends
Policy Advice	Nonpartisan experts	Political consultants, ideological think tanks
Public Opinion	Gain support across party lines	Polarized public
Media Relations	Cooperative; use broadcasting to reach mass public	Antagonistic use of "alternative media" or "partisan press" to reach niche publics
Electoral Politics	Candidate-centered politics; play down party affiliation; win support across party lines	Increasing polarization; revival of party organizations

Source: Richard Skinner, *The Partisan Presidency*, book manuscript (2013).

did in decades past. In electoral politics, presidents present partisan messages and rely on partisan and ideological allegiances among voters and activists to propel them to victory.

When governing, presidents now use the ample tools of the administrative presidency for partisan and ideological purposes. They seek to expand unilateral tools such as executive orders and signing statements for these ends as well. Policy guidance comes increasingly from partisan political consultants and ideological think tanks like the conservative Heritage Foundation and American Enterprise Institute (for Republican presidents) and the liberal Center for American Progress and Brookings Institution (for Democratic presidents).

All this adds up to a menu of presidential activities that strongly reinforces the ideological and partisan divide at the center of American politics. It began in the 1980s as Ronald Reagan governed as if on an ideological and partisan mission: "He sought to remake the Republican Party in his conservative image and to vault it into majority status. . . . Through centralization of policy decisions and appointment of ideological loyalists, Reagan managed to make the executive branch a tool of conservative governance" (Skinner 2013, 10,

16). Reagan also issued strictly conservative appointments to federal courts and aggressively courted sympathetic media outlets.

Republican George Herbert Walker Bush and his successor, Democrat Bill Clinton, at times attempted to govern from the center but frequently fell prey to partisan divides in public job approval and congressional voting. Both the conservative George W. Bush and the liberal Barack Obama, however, have emulated Reagan's approach.

Except during a brief period of national unity after the 9/11 attacks, George W. Bush proved highly polarizing through his partisan governing style. Bush pursued a muscular and controversial foreign policy by initiating wars in Afghanistan and Iraq. He successfully advocated federal tax cuts, a popular conservative policy. His prescription drug program for Medicare recipients and "No Child Left Behind" educational reforms spawned energetic opposition by liberal Democrats, who viewed them as inadequate responses to major national problems. Bush's executive and judicial appointments, like Reagan's, were uniformly conservative. He aggressively campaigned for GOP candidates and pursued a communications strategy that emphasized conservative media outlets such as talk radio and Fox News. His energetic use of unilateral presidential tools to pursue his policy agenda produced much partisan and ideological criticism from opponents.

Obama's initial calls for bipartisan unity were succeeded by a highly partisan governing style. From the outset of his presidency, Republicans voiced strong policy opposition to his domestic initiatives. His major early accomplishments of an economic "stimulus" plan, financial services reform, and the Affordable Care Act, his health services reform, passed Congress narrowly on party-line votes. Conservative opponents viewed them as fruitless "big government" initiatives. In 2010, 2012, and 2014, he campaigned emphatically for fellow Democrats and castigated his GOP opponents.

Barack Obama's agenda has been, for the most part, emphatically liberal: "Obama has been able to deliver on a remarkable array of progressive policy outcomes: a far-reaching economic stimulus package, greater regulation of financial markets, open service by gay, lesbian and bisexual people in the military, appointment of two liberal justices to the Supreme Court and, above all, the long-sought enactment of universal health coverage" (Skinner 2013). Like Bush, he undertook controversial unilateral actions to achieve his ends. In 2013, Obama delayed implementation of certain provisions of the Affordable Care Act for one year despite having no clear authority in the law to do so. He claimed the right to make "recess appointments" of individuals blocked from a Senate approval vote by GOP senators, a move that led to the Supreme Court ruling his action unconstitutional (Barnes 2014). In 2014, frustrated by congressional inaction on the issue, Obama's administration announced extensive new regulations aimed at curbing global warming (Davenport 2014).

Presidents behave in this way because they seek support where they can find it. They find it, in recent years, only on one side of a partisan and ideological divide that encompasses America's national politics. Chief executives, day to day, must build coalitions in support of their policies.

The partisan presidency resulted from the polarization and ideological realignment that has occurred in the American political system since 1980. The Republican Party has become more conservative, while the Democrat Party has become more liberal. "Views on a wide range of issues have become more closely tied to party identification than they were in the 1970s, as has religiosity. . . . Presidents have both helped to create this new political environment, and have to operate within it" (Skinner 2013, 18).

Political Weakness in the Partisan Presidency

While the presidency was becoming more ideological, it was also beginning to rest on a less secure foundation of political power. Since Ronald Reagan began his ideological presidency in 1980, presidents have suffered from lower levels of "political capital" than did most presidents during the period of the "modern presidency from 1932 to 1980. Political capital is the level of political support enjoyed by a president. Its components include (1) public approval of the president's performance in office, (2) the president's margin of victory in recent elections and (3) his party's support in Congress" (Light 1999, 15). A president ranking high on these indicators has high levels of political capital that can promote success in office.

Partisan presidents, however, rank lower than most "modern president" predecessors on several measures of political capital. Presidential victory margins in elections have shrunk. The last presidential landslide in the popular vote occurred in 1984 when Reagan defeated Walter Mondale. Since 1992, no winning president has received even 53 percent of the national vote. Partisan presidents have had lower net public approval, measured by subtracting the percentage of disapprovers from the percentage of approvers. FDR, Eisenhower, Kennedy, and Johnson all averaged net approval at +25 percent or more, but Reagan, George W. Bush, and Obama all rank below +15 percent due to the polarization attending their conduct of office. Reagan, Bush, and Obama's average job approval hovered around 50 percent, well below that of predecessors FDR, Eisenhower, Kennedy, and Johnson.

Partisan presidents also suffered from having smaller percentages of the public identifying with their parties. Democratic presidents FDR, Kennedy,

Johnson, and Carter had big advantages in this regard, with the percentage of their fellow partisans in the electorate average in the mid to high forties during their time in office. Reagan, George W. Bush, and Obama averaged below 40 percent in this measure. One consequence of ideological polarization has been an increase in the number of political independents who rejected full-throated GOP conservatism and Democratic liberalism. That has left partisan presidents with smaller partisan bases of support in the electorate.

The percentage of members of the House and Senate of the president's party is also lower for recent partisan presidents. Previous Democratic presidents FDR, Truman, Kennedy, Johnson, and Carter all had substantial Democratic majorities during most of their time in office, but Reagan, Bush, and Obama much of the time either had a hostile partisan majority in both chambers or split party control of the two chambers. It's no surprise that their levels of voting support for their agendas in Congress also was much lower than that of many of their predecessors (Schier and Eberly 2013, 90–91). A further investigation of the problems recent ideological presidents have faced with Congress will illustrate the political weaknesses of these chief executives.

Presidential–Congressional Conflicts

Presidents and members of Congress have very different perspectives regarding the state of the nation. Presidents consider the political and policy problems of the nation as a whole regarding foreign and domestic affairs. Members of the House and Senate, however, represent smaller geographical slices of the country and reflect the perspective of the people from their area who elected them to office. Presidents, due to these differences of perspective, frequently find garnering congressional support for their agenda one of the major challenges of their office.

Ideological polarization further limits the ability of presidents to persuade legislators for follow their lead. This polarization is the result of two trends. First, "the partisan, ideological and policy opinions of American voters have grown more internally consistent, more distinctive between parties, and more predictive of voting in national elections" (Jacobson 2013, 4). Second, the electorates of U.S. representatives and senators have become more homogeneously partisan (Levendusky 2009). Add the two together, and Congress becomes a group of liberal Democrats, conservative Republicans, and very few moderates of either party.

The root of the problem is evident in Figures 4.1 and 4.2. Geographical, partisan, and ideological polarizations have all combined to confine a president's electoral success to areas where his party also dominates congressional elections. In both the House and the Senate, few legislators of the rival party

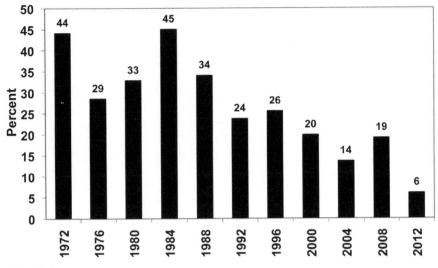

FIGURE 4.1
Districts with split results in presidential and House elections, 1972–2012.
Source: Gary C. Jacobson, *Partisan Polarization in American Politics: A Background Paper for Oxford Conference on Governing in Polarized Politics*, Balliol College, Oxford, April 16–17, 2013.

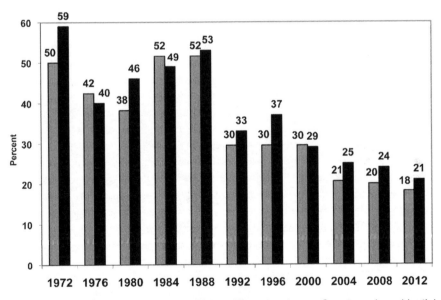

☐ Percentage of states in which a different party won Senate and presidential
majorities in the election

■ Percentage of all 100 senators who represented states lost by their party's
presidential candidate after the election

FIGURE 4.2
States with split results in Senate and presidential elections, 1972–2012.
Source: Gary C. Jacobson, *Partisan Polarization in American Politics: A Background Paper for Oxford Conference on Governing in Polarized Politics, Balliol College, Oxford Politics, Balliol College, Oxford, April 16–17, 2013.*

are from areas carried by the president. If a lawmaker's district opposes the president and the lawmaker represents the rival party in Congress, it is certain that on policy and ideology that legislator is distant from the White House. The number of lawmakers from the rival party in those circumstances has increased steadily since 1972. Figures 4.1 and 4.2 outline the limits of presidential support in Congress, and those limits have grown.

When an ideological president seeks support on Capitol Hill, then, he has few prospects of winning the support of the other party. If his party is in the minority, his prospects for legislative success are very dim, as happened to George W. Bush in 2007 and 2008 when none of his legislative agenda items became law. Even if the president's party controls one chamber, the rival chamber can obstruct the president's proposals. The GOP House since 2010, for example, has voted dozens of times to repeal the Affordable Care Act, a landmark liberal reform of President Obama.

Only when the president's party has majority control in both congressional chambers can ideological presidents prevail, as Bush did from 2003 to 2007 and Obama from 2009 to 2011. Both had very high levels of legislative success during those periods (media.cq.com 2013). That success is usually only possible if the president's party holds sixty of one hundred Senate seats, the number needed to stop a filibuster—unlimited debate—by members of the rival party. It is no surprise that the number of Senate filibusters have grown appreciably during the decades featuring an increasingly partisan and ideological presidency (Schier and Eberly 2013, 72).

Given frequent congressional obstruction, what is a president to do? Presidents in recent decades have increasingly "gone public" trying to move the legislature and public to support them through speeches and media appearances (Kernell 1997). This became a key strategy of Ronald Reagan's ideological and partisan presidency. In 2005, George W. Bush attempted to "go public" in advocating a major reform of Social Security, the federal government's major retirement system. Barack Obama spent several years trying to muster public support for his Affordable Care Act, his landmark health care reform.

Bush and Obama failed in their attempt to move public opinion. Why? "Most people ignore or reject arguments contrary to their predispositions. Nor can the president depend on those predisposed toward him to be especially responsive or to resist national trends opposed to the president's position. Presidents, then, find it very difficult to move the public. Usually they fail" (Edwards 2003, 238). With activists more polarized, going public is of limited use. Because of party sorting, those in the rival party are ideologically predisposed to ignore appeals. Those in the president's party are likely already onboard. Those who are not ideologically inclined do not respond to partisan or ideological appeals and are less likely to be listening in the first place (Prior 2007).

Why do presidents engage in such persuasion, then? Because bargaining with Congress will not work—the battle lines are drawn there between conservative Republicans and liberal Democrats and it is a "no man's land" between them.

So going public is the best "long shot" bet, for three reasons. First, presidents were elected by going public and know how to do it. It is a ready skill. Second, going public can maintain existing support, which is always politically helpful. Third, going public may influence elite opinion and get the media to circulate the president's message. Elite pressure from D.C. interest groups and national media may follow that can help the president in Congress (Edwards 2003, 242–46). However, long shots seldom pay off. "To the extent that polarization creates incentives to avoid bargaining in favor of going public, polarization may be pushing presidents toward failure" (Newman and Siegle 2010, 361).

One way around Congress, of course, is through presidential use of unilateral tools. Divided government and ideological and partisan polarization encourage presidents to act unilaterally by "shifting the locus of government policymaking away from lawmaking and towards executive and administrative action" (Devins 2009, 411). Unilateral action, as we will see, carries its own political costs. We next turn to the administrative tools presidents use to further their ideological agendas, given their frustrations with Congress—management of executive agencies and bureaucratic and judicial appointments.

Administrative Tools for Ideological Ends

Both George W. Bush and Barack Obama followed Ronald Reagan's example in placing a partisan and ideological cast on their administration of the executive branch. Bush and Obama, like Reagan, selected ideologically sympathetic subordinates, centralized policy and personnel decisions in the White House, and used the Office of Management and Budget to enforce presidential plans for the bureaucracy. Bush, for example, sought to curb the power of public employee unions, a Democratic constituency. He had regulatory agencies create offices staffed by political appointees to oversee bureaucratic rulemaking. He also sought "greater partisan/ideological control of the judiciary, by creating recruitment processes that emphasized philosophy as much as competence of political connections" (Skinner 2008, 616).

Barack Obama's presidency turned into "a generic Democratic administration of the partisan era" (Skinner 2013, 19). His administration was populated by former Democratic officeholders and by people from liberal think tanks such as the Center for American Progress. He directed regulatory agencies such as the Food and Drug Administration and Environmental Protection Agency to be far more aggressive than they had been under Bush, who had restrained them. His White House viewed enhanced regulation as a form of "party building" by rewarding liberal interest groups and consolidating their support for his approach (Milkis, Rhodes, and Charnock 2012). As we see in the next chapter, his judicial appointments were as reliably liberal as those of George W. Bush were conservative.

The federal bureaucracy is home to a variety of ideological dispositions among its employees. Recent political science research has identified the most conservative and liberal agencies. A survey of agency executives found the most conservative worked for the Department of Defense, Army, Navy, and Air Force and Department of Homeland Security. The most liberal executives labored in the National Labor Relations Board (NLRB), Environmental Protection Agency (EPA), Federal Trade Commission, and Department of Health and Human Services (Clinton et al. 2011, 349). The agenda of partisan presidents George W. Bush and Barack Obama put their ideologically favored agencies in the spotlight. Defense funding surged during the Bush presidency as it prosecuted the "war on terror" in Afghanistan, Iraq, and globally. Bush supported the creation of the large Department of Homeland Security. Barack Obama's energetic approach to regulation thrust the EPA and NLRB into controversy as they drew harsh censure from conservative critics. Senate Republicans refused to confirm several Obama nominees to the NLRB because of their "pro-union" agenda. Senate Republicans in 2013 also delayed the appointment of EPA director Gina McCarthy in 2013 due to her outspoken environmentalism. The Department of Health and Human Services and its secretary, Kathleen Sibelius, became political targets of conservatives as the department began implementation of the highly controversial Affordable Care Act.

Conclusion: Problems and Dangers

America's recent partisan and ideological presidents have encountered fewer fellow partisans and less voting support in both the public and Congress and less popular approval of their job performance and party than did their predecessors. The decline in their political capital has produced great difficulties for presidential leadership in recent decades. It is difficult to exert leadership in an era when job approval, congressional support, and partisan affiliation provide less backing for a president than in times past.

Because of the uncertainties of political capital, recent presidents have adopted a governing style that is personalized, preemptive, and, at times, isolated. Given the entrenched autonomy of other elite actors and the impermanence of public opinion, presidents have had to "sell themselves" in order to sell their governance, "going public" as a response to these conditions. This has not improved their public and congressional support.

The modern presidency, however, grants an incumbent several formal powers over executive branch administration and foreign and national security policy. Moreover, if persuasion does not work with the public and Congress because political capital is meager, why not just assert power? Power exertion via unilateral decisions and signing statements and executive orders is tempting for presidents in such circumstances. Such exertions often receive much media attention due to the conflict they create, and conflict can be politically costly to presidents. The risk is that by using such powers, a president effectively can further erode his political capital. That is the political power trap.

Ideological presidents have at times fallen into the power trap. Ronald Reagan gradually relied more on executive power as his political capital declined in his second term, leading to the Iran-Contra imbroglio. The Reagan administration engaged in an arms-for-hostages negotiation with Iran that violated federal law, a unilateral action undertaken apparently without the president's knowledge. George H. W. Bush and Bill Clinton at times tried to govern less ideologically, but gradually suffered a political capital shortage and found their use of powers under steady political attack. George W. Bush's unilateral use of war powers destroyed what political capital remained by the end of his second term.

Barack Obama's political capital problems also prompted unilateral presidential actions. We have already mentioned his controversial recess appointments now under federal court challenge and his postponement of provisions of the Affordable Care Act that apparently has no basis in the law itself. Furthermore, in 2012, President Obama relied on executive discretion and legal ambiguity to allow homeowners to more easily refinance federally backed mortgages, to help veterans find employment, and to make it easier for college graduates to consolidate federal student-loan debt and placing caps on federal student-loan payments (Savage 2012). President Obama even used an executive order to authorize the Department of Education to grant states waivers from the requirements of the No Child Left Behind Act—though the enacting legislation makes no accommodation for such waivers. President Obama also sought to expand his powers by appointing "czars" to carry out special tasks for the president.

By his second term, Obama's job approval had slipped well below its initial levels, and Congress was proving increasingly intransigent. In the face of declining public support and rising congressional opposition, Obama, like his predecessors when faced with similar circumstances, continued to resort to the energetic use of executive power. Declining political capital and accompanying assertions of executive power—we have seen this movie before.

On July 2, 2014, two headlines appeared on Internet political news sites. At yahoo.com news: "Obama vows to act alone" indicating his intention to act unilaterally whenever possible and taunting his opponents with the assertion "so sue me" (Kuhnhenn and Werner 2014). A second headline featured the results of a new Quinnipiac national survey: "Poll Ranks Obama as Worst President Since WWII," ominous news indeed for the White House. Thirty-three respondents ranked Obama worst, followed closely by George W. Bush, whom 28 percent ranked at the bottom (Jackson 2014).

These trends—presidential unilateralism and low presidential popularity—are strongly related. Obama faced a political capital problem and a power trap. Those two headlines from the same day illustrated the phenomena perfectly.

As Obama discovered, unilateral actions by ideological presidents often produce Constitutional controversies and can land a president in even deeper political problems. Not only will partisan opponents contest such power assertions, but also public support of the president can drop. In recent years, citizens have reported greater ideological distance between themselves and presidents, which probably contributes to today's widespread popular distrust of national government (Hetherington 2006).

The only alternative to this troubling scenario lies in united government, in which one party controls both the legislature and the executive. That seems unlikely in the near future. "The prognosis, then, is for a continuation of divided government featuring ideologically polarized partisan conflict, because the current configuration of national politics reflects electoral realities that are unlikely to change soon" (Jacobson 2013, 20). Partisan redistricting had made the U.S. House a Republican stronghold while control of the Senate and presidency remained competitive between the parties.

Given the great ideological distance between Republicans and Democrats in Washington, bargaining between the parties to solve pressing national problems has become unlikely. Polarization discourages bargaining and encourages "going public" with ideological messages. That forces presidents to try enlisting the public in pressuring politicians in Washington, an approach that seldom if ever works.

So the alternative becomes the unilateral exercise of powers, courting new controversy and political opposition. A result is the power trap, when frustrated presidents overreach in grabbing unilateral powers and send their presidencies on a downward spiral. It has happened before, and may be even more likely when ideological presidents run into intractable partisan opposition.

The impact of the ideological presidency becomes evident when we examine how George W. Bush and Barack Obama have performed in important presidential roles. Both had sharply contrasting visions of America's role in the world and operated as commander-in-chief and leader of allied nations in accord with those visions. Bush's aggressive military actions in Iraq and Afghanistan heightened ideological and partisan divisions among Americans. Obama's foreign and military policies, far more muted than those of Bush, have aroused criticism from the American right just as Bush's policies riled the American left. The presidents' conduct in the role of chief executive also proved divisive. Big ideological and partisan divisions accompanied their major policy proposals—such as Bush's 2005 Social Security reform and Obama's 2009 health care proposal. Both presidents also used unilateral power such as executive orders and signing statements to enforce policies opposed by their ideological and partisan opponents. That furthered American political divisions as well.

Bush and Obama have functioned rhetorically as emphatic party leaders, seeking to maintain their partisan "base" support even as their policies became less popular over time with the broader public. One result was a record partisan "approval gap" encountered by both presidents. Rather than unify the public, both divided citizens by party and ideology.

When a president speaks and acts ideologically, he creates a large impact upon America's politics. Political debate becomes polarized and ideological divisions come to occupy national attention. At present, the presidency is a primary driver of ideology's importance in American politics. Heightened ideological conflict, brought to the fore by Bush and Obama, may well be the "new normal" of American politics.

References

Bafumi, Joseph, and Robert Y. Shapiro. 2009. "A New Partisan Voter." *Journal of Politics* 71 (1): 1–24.

Barnes, Robert. 2014. "Supreme Court rebukes Obama on recess appointments." *Washington Post.* June 26. http://www.washingtonpost.com/politics/supreme-court-rebukes-obama-on-recess-appointments/2014/06/26/e5e4fefa-e831-11e3-a86b-362fd5443d19_story.html (accessed July 2, 2014).

Bawm, Kathleen, Martin Cohen, David Karol, Seth Market, Hans Noel, and John Zaller. 2012. "A Theory of Political Parties: Groups, Policy Demands and Nominations in American Politics." *Perspectives on Politics* 10 (3): 571–97.

Burden, Barry C., and D. Sunshine Hillygus. 2009. "Opinion Formation, Polarization and Presidential Reelection." *Presidential Studies Quarterly* 39 (3): 619–35.

Clinton, Joshua D., Anthony Bertelli, Christian R. Grose, David E. Lewis, and David C. Nixon. 2011. "Separated Powers in the United States: The Ideology of Agencies, Presidents and Congress." *American Journal of Political Science* 56 (2): 341–54.

Congressional Quarterly. 2013. "Congressional Vote Studies." http://media.cq.com/blog/2013/01/vote-studies/ (accessed August 6, 2013).

Davenport, Coral. 2013. "Obama to Take Action to Slash Coal Pollution." *New York Times.* June 1. http://www.nytimes.com/2014/06/02/us/politics/epa-to-seek-30-percent-cut-in-carbon-emissions.html?_r=0 (accessed July 2, 2014).

Devins, Neal. 2009. "Presidential Unilateralism and Political Polarization: Why Today's Congress Lacks the Will and the Way to Stop Presidential Initiatives." *Willamette Law Review* 45:395–415.

Dorning, Mike, and Alex Wayne. 2013. "Health Care Employer Mandate Delayed by U.S. until 2015." *Bloomberg News.* July 3. http://www.bloomberg.com/news/2013-07-02/health-law-employer-mandate-said-to-be-delayed-to-2015.html (accessed August 6, 2013).

Edwards, George C. III. 2003. *On Deaf Ears: The Limits of the Bully Pulpit.* New Haven, CT: Yale University Press.

Fiorina, Morris C., and Samuel J. Abrams. 2009. *Disconnect: The Breakdown of Representation in American Politics.* Norman: University of Oklahoma Press.

Hetherington, Marc J. 2006. *Why Trust Matters: Declining Political Trust and the Demise of Political Liberalism.* Princeton, NJ: Princeton University Press.

Jackson, David. 2014. "Poll: Obama 'Worst President' since World War II." *USA Today.* July 2. http://www.usatoday.com/story/theoval/2014/07/02/obama-george-w-bush-quinnipiac-poll-reagan-clinton/11985837/ (accessed July 2, 2014).

Jacobson, Gary C. 2013. "Partisan Polarization in American Politics: A Background Paper for Oxford Conference on Governing in Polarized Politics." Balliol College, Oxford. April 16–17, 2013.

Jacoby, William. 2009. "Ideology and Vote Choice in the 2004 Election." *Electoral Studies* 28:584–94.

———. 2010. "Policy Attitudes, Ideology and Voting Behavior in the 2008 Election." *Electoral Studies* 29:557–68.

Jones, Jeffrey M. 2013. "Obama's Fourth Year in Office Ties as Most Polarized Ever." Gallup.com. January 24. http://www.gallup.com/poll/160097/obama-fourth-year-office-ties-polarized-ever.aspx (accessed August 6, 2013).

Kernell, Samuel. 1997. *Going Public: New Strategies of Presidential Leadership.* Washington DC: Congressional Quarterly Press.

Kuhnhenn, Jim, and Erica Werner. 2014. "Obama to Go It Alone on Immigration, Pleasing Few." Yahoo News. news.yahoo.com/obama-alone-immigration-pleasing-few-071256408—politics.html (accessed July 2, 2014).

Levendusky, Matthew. 2009. *The Partisan Sort: How Liberals Became Democrats and Conservatives Became Republicans.* Chicago: University of Chicago Press.

Light, Paul C. 1999. *The President's Agenda: Domestic Policy Choice from Kennedy to Clinton.* Baltimore, MD: Johns Hopkins University Press.

Media.cq.com. 2013. "2012 Congressional Vote Studies." *CQRollCall.* January 30. http://media.cq.com/blog/2013/01/vote-studies (accessed December 2, 2015).

Milkis, Sidney M., Jesse H. Rhodes, and Emily J. Charnock. 2012. "What Happened to Postpartisanship? Barack Obama and the New American Party System." *Perspectives on Politics* 10 (1): 57–76.

Mitchell, Alison. 2000. "The 2000 Campaign: The Texas Governor; Bush Says Gore Would Endanger Prosperity." *New York Times.* November 1. http://www.nytimes

.com/2000/10/19/us/2000-campaign-texas-governor-bush-says-gore-s-election
-would-endanger-prosperity.html?ref=alisonmitchell (accessed August 6, 2013).

Newman, Brian, and Emerson Siegel. 2010. "The Polarized Presidency: Depth and
Breadth of Public Partisanship." *Presidential Studies Quarterly* 40 (2): 342–63.

Nivola, Pietro. 2005. "Thinking about Political Polarization." Brookings Institution
Policy Brief. January. Washington, D.C.: Brookings Institution.

Prior, Markus. 2007. *Post-Broadcast Democracy: How Media Choice Increases Inequality in Political Involvement and Polarizes Elections.* Cambridge: Cambridge
University Press.

Rossiter, Clinton. 2012. "The Presidency—Focus of Leadership." In Peter Woll, ed.,
American Government: Readings and Cases, 267–72. 19th ed. Boston: Longman.

Savage, Charlie. 2012. "Shift on Executive Power Lets Obama Bypass Rivals." *New
York Times.* April 22. http://www.nytimes.com/2012/04/23/us/politics/shift-on-
executive-powers-let-obama-bypass-congress.html?pagewanted=all (accessed August 6, 2013).

Schier, Steven E., and Todd E. Eberly. 2013. *American Government and Popular Discontent: Stability without Success.* New York: Routledge.

Seelye, Katharine Q. 2001. "The President's Decision: The Overview: Bush Gives His
Backing for Limited Research on Existing Stem Cells." *New York Times.* August
10. http://www.nytimes.com/2001/08/10/us/president-s-decision-overview-bush-
gives-his-backing-for-limited-research.html?pagewanted=all&src=pm (accessed
August 6, 2013).

Shear, Michael D., and Peter Baker. 2013. "Obama Focuses on Economy, Vow-
ing to Help Middle Class." *New York Times.* July 24. http://www.nytimes
.com/2013/07/25/us/politics/obama-to-restate-economic-vision-at-knox-college
.html (accessed August 6, 2013).

Skinner, Richard. 2009. "George W. Bush and the Partisan Presidency." *Political Science Quarterly* 123 (4): 605–22. http://works.bepress.com/richard_skinner/8.

———. 2013. "The Partisan Presidency." Unpublished manuscript.

5

An Ideological Congress

I N JULY OF 1965, THE U.S. CONGRESS APPROVED what was then the most sweeping reform to the American health care system, the creation of Medicare to provide health care for Americans over the age of sixty-five, and the creation of Medicaid to provide health care for poor children and low-income pregnant women. It should come as no surprise that the battle over the creation of Medicare and Medicaid was contentious. Though the bill enjoyed the clear support of Democratic president Lyndon Johnson as well as Democratic leaders in Congress, there were deep pockets of opposition in the House and Senate. At the time, Congress was dominated by the Democratic Party, as had been the case for most of the Congresses since the election of Franklin Roosevelt in 1932. The Democrats' advantage in the House and Senate was so substantial that no Republican support was needed to pass the bill.

The legislation creating Medicare and Medicaid was drafted by the House Committee on Ways and Means. Though Democrats dominated the committee, the committee chair, Wilbur Mills, preferred to avoid confrontational or divisive votes on the floor of the House. So Mills negotiated with the Republican ranking member on the committee, John Byrnes, to craft the legislation. Rather than use his majority power to push through President Johnson's version of the bill, Mills' committee ultimately produced legislation that combined elements of Johnson's bill with an alternate bill proposed by Byrnes. On the floor, the legislation was subject to roughly five hundred amendments before finally passing by a vote of 307-117 in the House and 70-24 in the Senate. The lopsided majorities included over 50 percent of House Republicans and more than 40 percent of Senate Republicans (Evans 2012). Times have certainly changed.

Students of contemporary American politics may recall a more recent sweeping reform to the American health care system, the Patient Protection and Affordable Care Act, or *ObamaCare*, passed by the House and Senate in March of 2010. Observers of the congressional debates and partisan wrangling over the Patient Protection and Affordable Care Act are likely aware of the contentious battle that led up to the final passage of the bill without a single Republican vote.

The legislation creating the Affordable Care Act was largely crafted by Democratic Party leadership outside of the congressional committee process. Though Senator Max Baucus, the moderate Democrat who chaired the Senate Finance Committee, briefly attempted to craft a bill that would attract at least the support of minority committee member Olympia Snowe, a moderate Republican, Senate Majority Leader Harry Reid ultimately instructed Baucus to give up the effort and opted for a partisan bill with no chance of Republican support. In the House, Democratic Speaker Nancy Pelosi instructed the chairs of the three committees with jurisdiction (each hand-picked by Pelosi) over the legislation to craft a bill together before involving their committee members. Leadership remained an active voice in crafting the legislation, and when progress in the Energy and Commerce Committee was delayed by the concerns of moderate Democrats, committee Chair Henry Waxman threatened to bypass his own committee and take the leadership's legislation directly to the House floor for a vote (Sinclair 2012).

The final votes on the Affordable Care Act were demonstrably different from those approving the creation of Medicare and Medicaid. In the House, Democratic Party leadership was worried about the possible defection of moderate Democrats over issues like abortion coverage. To prevent Republicans from undermining Democratic Party unity by offering amendments that would exploit Democratic divisions, the House Rules Committee (with a chair picked by Speaker Pelosi) sent the bill to the floor of the House with a closed rule. A closed rule severely restricts what can happen on the floor during consideration of the bill. The rule precluded Republicans from offering any amendments save for a single motion to recommit—a legislative procedure in which the bill is sent back to committee to correct some perceived flaw or oversight. In the Senate, the final version of the bill was considered using a procedural tactic known as reconciliation. Created to ensure the passage of crucial budgeting legislation, the reconciliation process precludes filibusters and requires a simple majority vote to approve legislation.

Two pieces of legislation, both introducing fundamental reforms to American health care policy, both supported by a president and a congressional majority of fellow partisans, and both contentious. Yet one followed a traditional path of committee development and amendment on the floor before receiving considerable bipartisan support. The other bypassed the once-normal legislative process, was crafted largely by leadership, excluded the minority party, and limited the input of rank-and-file members of the majority party before receiving approval by a party-line vote in the House and the Senate. What can explain the very different paths taken by these two pieces of legislation? The answer lies in dramatic changes in the ideological makeup of Congress that took place during the intervening decades. These changes witnessed a dramatic decline in the share of representatives and senators amassed near the political center and the emergence of a very polarized institution.

A Call for More Responsible Parties

Those familiar with the partisan gridlock that defines the modern Congress can be forgiven should they look fondly upon the bygone days of bipartisan cooperation in Congress. Political scientists lament as well the current state of Congressional dysfunction (Fiorina and Abrams 2009). But in the years prior to the passage of the Medicare and Medicaid legislation, political scientists were lamenting the lack of partisanship and the presence of too much bipartisan cooperation that often blurred the distinctions between Republicans and Democrats. Concern was so great that the American Political Science Association (APSA) formed a special panel on political parties tasked with studying ways to make parties more effective. The resulting report, "Toward a More Responsible Two-Party System: A Report of the Committee on Political Parties," was released in 1950.

At that time, there was tremendous partisan and ideological overlap in the Congress. Though Democrats dominated national politics, the congressional agenda was often controlled by a coalition of conservative southern Democrats and Republicans. Rather than two national political parties, Democrats and Republicans were more akin to coalitions of regional parties—often with divergent interests. The Democratic Party was divided between northern liberal members and southern conservatives. The Republican coalition included moderate northern Republicans and more conservative Midwest and western members. This intra-party diversity made national policymaking more difficult. "As a result, either major party, when in power, is ill-equipped to organize its members in the legislative and the executive branches into a government held together and guided by the party program" (APSA 1950, p.v.).

Perhaps of greater concern, the lack of party cohesion and distinction introduced serious accountability challenges. How could the public make an informed choice in an election if a Democrat in one region of the country could not be counted on to share the beliefs and goals of a Democrat elected in another region of the country? The report recommended stronger and more ideologically consistent political parties. They envisioned parties that were "able to bring forth programs to which they commit themselves and . . . possess sufficient internal cohesion to carry out these programs" (APSA 1950, 17–18).

The authors concluded the weak party system of the time was a barrier to effective democratic leadership. Only parties could bridge the divide between policymakers and the public because they were able to reach people in a way unmatched by any other political organization. Voters needed a party system in which a majority party proposes and pursues its clearly enunciated agenda while the opposition or minority party serves as critic of the majority, developing, defining, and presenting policy alternatives that offer voters a true choice.

In Congress, the APSA panel advocated party unity and means by which to enforce party discipline. In other words, Democratic members of Congress should support the policies put forth in the Democratic Party platform and Republican members should stand as the loyal opposition and offer their own distinct policies. The authors dismissed concerns that such ideologically distinct parties might lead to deep division among the electorate, noting "There is no real ideological division in the American electorate, and hence programs of action presented by responsible parties for the voter's support could hardly be expected to reflect or strive toward such division" (APSA 1950, 20–21).

Too Much of a Good Thing

Most observers of the contemporary Congress would conclude that the APSA panel on political parties got much of what it wanted. The parties today are more clearly defined and associated with distinct and typically opposing policy preferences. Consider the evolution of the party platforms regarding the issue of abortion as presented in chapter 2. Certainly there can be little doubt today as to which party supports abortion rights and which party opposes it. And, unlike decades past, party members typically endorse the sentiments contained in the party platform—even if it means allowing one's beliefs to evolve.

Party unity in Congress has been achieved as well. Party unity refers to the percentage of House or Senate votes on which a member voted in agreement with a majority of his or her own party. Figures 5.1 and 5.2 show average party unity scores in the House and the Senate, respectively, from 1956 through 2013 as measured by *Congressional Quarterly*. In 2013, House Republicans set

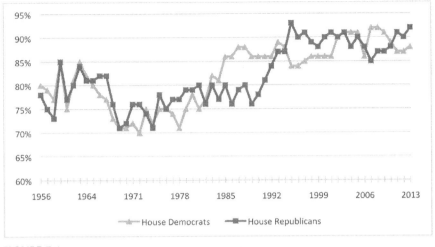

FIGURE 5.1
Average party unity scores, House.

a record for party support, voting on average with their caucus 95 percent of the time. Likewise, Senate Democrats set a record, raising their average party unity score to 94 percent from the previous record of 92 percent.

Beyond party unity, there is clear ideological cohesion among the two parties. Figure 5.3 compares the ideological distribution of Democratic and

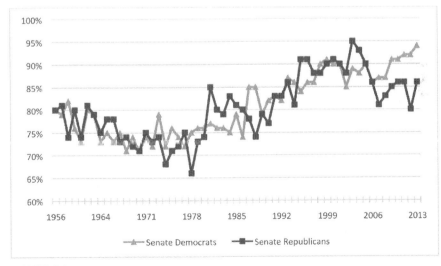

FIGURE 5.2
Average party unity scores, Senate.

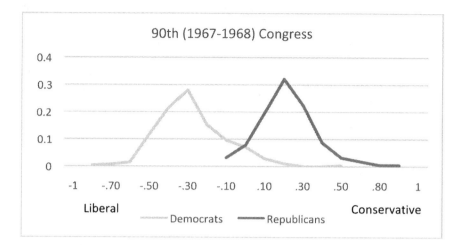

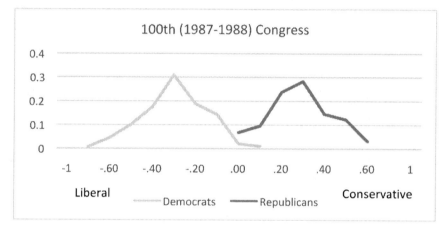

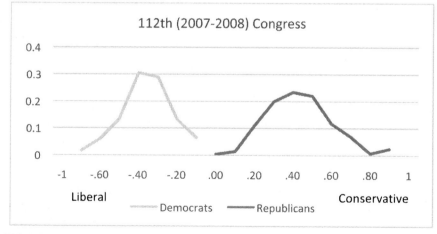

FIGURE 5.3
Ideological distribution of party members in Congress.

Republican members of Congress at three points during a forty-year period between 1967 and 2008. What they reveal is a Congress with ever-fewer moderate or centrist members. While it was once common to have Democratic members more conservative than many Republican members and many Republicans more liberal than many Democratic members, the amount of overlap has been shrinking since the 1960s. A review of members in the 112th Congress in 2007–2008 revealed that no overlap existed.

The emergence of clearly distinct parties in Congress produced significant changes in the day-to-day operations of the House and Senate—most notably, the concentration of power among party leadership and the steady erosion of once common practices. The U.S. Constitution has little to say about the day-to-day operations of Congress. Rather, it is left to each chamber to develop its own rules and procedures. At the time of the APSA report on parties, there was a significant amount of ideological overlap among members of Congress regardless of party. Given this level of ideological diversity, members were reluctant to cede too much agenda control to party leadership as they may pursue policies that are contrary to the member's preference. But as the two parties became more ideologically homogenous and the distance between their ideologies grew larger, members became more willing to empower leadership.

According to the theory of *conditional party government,* if a party has diverse policy preferences, members will not grant strong power to party leadership. However, homogenous policy preferences lead to an empowered leadership. This tendency is enhanced as the positions of the two parties become more divergent (Aldrich and Rohde 2009). The cause of this comes down to the consequences of loss. If the parties hold deep ideological differences, they are likely to pursue fundamentally different policies. As such, the price of losing a legislative battle would be quite high. By centralizing power in party leadership, members increase their party's strength—*united we stand, divided we fall.*

As the parties diverged ideologically and became more internally cohesive after the late 1960s, congressional rules and procedures were reformed to give greater power to leadership. As the distance between the two parties continued to widen, majority party leadership responded by finding ways to bypass the minority. In the Senate, where unlimited debate has long been a hallmark of the institution, the number of votes needed to end a filibuster was lowered from two-thirds (sixty-seven) to three-fifths (sixty) in 1975. During the same time period, the Speaker of the House gained the authority to determine the majority party membership of the Rules Committee. This meant the speaker gained control of the terms of debate for legislation on the House floor. Increasingly, rules were imposed that severely restricted or even eliminated any opportunity to amend legislation. There was a ten-fold increase in the share of major legislation subject to restrictive rules between the 89th Congress in 1966 and the 110th in 2008. During the same period, the number of days in session and the number of committee and subcommittee meetings fell dramatically. Legislation was increasingly subject to change by party leadership outside of the committee process. All of these changes worked to minimize the influence and input of minority party members (Schier and Eberly 2013).

Relegated to the sidelines, minority party members sought ways to obstruct the process (Schier and Eberly 2013). Minority Republicans took advantage of recorded votes and the presence of television cameras in the House and Senate chambers by forcing Democrats in competitive districts to cast votes against politically popular amendments. In the Senate, minority Republicans and then minority Democrats made increasing use of the filibuster to derail legislation (Schier and Eberly 2013). These tactics, coupled with an ongoing decline on the number of members who bridged the ideological divide between the two parties, served to bolster a sense of mistrust and even animosity between the parties.

Causes of the Ideological Polarization in Congress

So what brought about the ideological sorting of the two parties? Though no single change or event can explain the rise of ideologically rigid parties, political scientists do agree on some of the contributing factors. In the Democratic Party, ideological diversity was very much an artifact of Reconstruction-era politics. Though the party was home to a growing number of moderate to liberal voters in the Northeast, it had long been dominated by conservative southern Democrats. In the South, Republicans were long viewed as the party of the Civil War and Reconstruction. When Republicans ended Reconstruction and withdrew federal troops from the South in the late 1870s, conservative Democrats regained control. What emerged were the decades of Jim Crow, poll taxes, literacy tests, and white primaries all employed to deny African Americans political representation. For much of the time between the end of Reconstruction and the late 1960s, there was virtually no Republican presence in the South.

As liberal northern Democrats, along with liberal Democratic presidents John Kennedy and Lyndon Johnson, aggressively pursued civil rights legislation, the politics of the South began to change. The Voting Rights Act of 1965 stripped away many of the impediments long placed before African Americans in the South. As more African Americans registered and voted, conservative Democrats were defeated in primaries or retired and were replaced by more liberal Democrats. To counter the emergence of liberal Democrats, southern conservatives looked to the Republican Party and the number of conservative southern Republicans grew steadily. The Democratic

Party's support of civil rights attracted the support of African Americans who had escaped the South and migrated to urban centers in the North, as well as younger voters and better-educated voters. Many of these voters supported other more-liberal causes such as environmental protection and equal rights for women. The Democratic Party responded by adopting these issues in an effort to bolster party strength. As the Republicans' base shifted to more conservative southern voters, the party agenda became more conservative and Republicans found greater support among voters uncomfortable with the social changes associated with the Democratic Party. As the nature of each party's voting coalition changed, the parties changed as well.

As odd as may seem, the advent of air conditioning and suburban sprawl had an impact on the ideological development of the parties. Indoor air conditioning, which made the hot southern and southwestern summers bearable, facilitated a mass migration of Americans from the industrial areas of the Northeast and Midwest. These Americans tended to be older, white, and conservative. A significant number of electoral votes and seats in the House of Representatives followed these voters (Fiorina and Abrams 2009). In addition to migration to new regions of the country, voters began to spread out from the population centers, and levels of civic engagement declined. In his book *Bowling Alone*, Robert Putnam documents the decline of membership in community groups like the Rotary Club, as well as decreased time spent with friends, neighbors, and family and a decline in voter turnout (Putman 2001). In the absence of cohesive communities and general membership organizations, it became more of a challenge for candidates and elected official to make contact with voters. New methods for contacting and motivating members were needed. The rise of special interest groups, such as the National Rifle Association, the Sierra Club, and the National Organization for Women, offered one way to reach voters. Candidates could win the support of special-interest groups and rely on group members for support (Fiorina and Abrams 2009). But special-interest groups tend to be single-issue groups (gun rights, environmental protection) and they preferred to support candidates who passionately endorsed their agenda—which was not a recipe for moderation.

By the 1980s, Republicans had secured a foothold in the South and the once-dominant Democratic Party was faced with serious competition for control of the federal government. Ronald Reagan was elected president in 1980 and Republicans won control of the U.S. Senate for the first time since the 1950s—largely as a result of victories in southern states. In the face of increased party competition, political parties responded by bolstering efforts to motivate their core supporters, which meant liberal voters for Democrats and conservative voters for Republicans. Daniel Coffey, via an examination of state party platforms, found a positive correlation between party competition and party polarization. As a state becomes more competitive between Republicans and Democrats, the parties respond by becoming ever-more conservative and liberal (Coffey 2011). The evolution of the national party platform statements on abortion, discussed in chapter 3, is an effective demonstration of the phenomenon.

The manner in which congressional districts are drawn played a role as well, though political scientists disagree over the significance of that role. In most states, the drawing of congressional districts lines is completed by elected officials such as the governor, the state legislature, or both. The advent of advanced computer modeling and mapping allowed for the creation of districts that advantaged the party in charge of the process, a practice typically referred to as gerrymandering. Democrats could divide Republican areas among multiple congressional districts in an effort to minimize their voting power. Republicans could pack Democrats into one or a just a few districts to achieve the same goal, the result of either approach being safe partisan districts. In the House of Representatives today, it is estimated that only about fifty to sixty of the chamber's 435 seats are actually competitive. In the absence of electoral competition, there is little pressure on elected officials to seek moderation. Gerrymandering can in turn influence polarization in the Senate as House members seek higher office (Theriault and Rohde 2011).

Primaries can contribute to ideologically polarized parties as well, regardless of gerrymandering. Since the early 1970s, primaries have become the most common way to nominate candidates for office. Though a candidate may be safe in the general election, he or she may face a serious challenge from within his or her own party during a primary. In most states, primaries are closed to all but registered members of the party holding the primary. As such, there is little motivation for a candidate to embrace moderation. Turnout is generally lower in primary elections and primary voters tend to prefer more ideological extreme candidates (Brady, Han, and Pope 2007; Jacobson 2012). Campaigns are also quite expensive and victory often hinges on a candidate's ability to raise sufficient funds. Though special-interest groups are important, individual contributions are the main source of campaign funds. A relatively small segment of the electorate is responsible for most campaign contributions and those who do contribute money tend to be more ideologically extreme than those who do not (Bafumi and Herron 2009). So it should come as no surprise that the more conservative (liberal) a Republican (Democratic) candidate is relative to other candidates the more money he or she will raise from individuals. Raising funds and winning primaries is so difficult for moderate candidates that they often opt to not run for Congress (Thompsen 2014), surrendering the playing field to more ideological candidates.

The need for money encourages ideological division in other ways as well. Even as congressional members were entrusting ever more power in party leadership, those leaders tended to be "ideological middlemen," meaning that they were closer to the ideological center of their party membership than to either of the wings. Such party centrists were chosen as they were viewed as being less likely to put their own partisan interests ahead of the party and per- haps foster divisions within the party (Cox and McCubbins 1993). A review of elected party leaders in Congress between 1981 and 1991 found that party centrists outnumbered party extremists by a margin of two to one. However, the same review conducted between 1993 and 2003 found that the numbers had flipped: party extremists outnumbered centrists by two to one.

What caused the dramatic shift in leadership preference? Money. As party competition increased and campaigns grew ever-more expensive, party members who were able to raise substantial amounts of money became more crucial. Members who are especially good at raising money are able to redistribute that money to other races. To the extent that they shift their money to closely fought races, their contributions become invaluable to maintaining control of the chamber. Between 1991 and 2001, the amount of campaign money redistributed by members to other members increased from $3 million to $40 million, and among those members elected to leadership positions between 1993 and 2003, the overwhelming majority came from the most-extreme third of party membership and were the biggest redistribu- tors of money. If elected leaders become more extreme, then members of the party's extended leadership are likely to become more extreme as well given that elected leaders appoint members to the party's extended leadership posts (Heberlig, Hetherington, and Larson 2006).

And what do party leaders do with their power? It turns out they promote ideological division and polarization within Congress. Majority party leaders control the agenda, as such they decide what will be considered as well as what will not be. In order to promote party unity and minimize within-party divisions, party leaders rarely bring to the floor any measure that does not enjoy majority support from the majority party. In other words, leadership rarely allows votes on a measure if a majority of their party would vote against it. By selecting measures that promote majority party unity, leadership inevi- tably promotes minority party unity in opposition (Evans 2012).

There is little to suggest that many members of the minority party would support a measure tailored to the median member of the majority party and not to the median member of the House or Senate. Leadership promotes ideological division as well by limiting the ability to amend legislation. In the House, the Rules Committee may limit the minority party to a single amendment (or no amendment) and even specify which amendments can be offered. In the Senate, the majority leader enjoys the right to offer the first amendments to a bill and may, if he or she so chooses, claim all available opportunities for amendment. When the minority party has an opportunity to offer an amendment, its leadership will likewise pursue a measure acceptable to a majority of the minority party membership. As a result, majority and minority party members are presented with two polarized options, one tailored to the median member of the majority party and one tailored to the median member of the minority party, the likely outcome being two unified parties voting in opposite directions (Evans 2012).

Ideological Intransigence and National Policymaking

The extent of the division present in Congress becomes evident with only a cursory review of recent news. The United States adopted legislation establishing a general limit on federal debt in 1939. The legislation sought to minimize deficit spending and federal borrowing to cover the spending approved in the federal budget. In the years and decades that followed, Congress routinely passed legislation to raise or waive the limit. The limit was increased every year between 1941 and 1945 as the costs of financing U.S. involvement in World War II escalated (Austin and Levit 2013). Congress approved changes to the debt limit seventy-seven times between 1962 and 2013—an average of one and a half changes per year. Debt limit increases became commonplace and were approved during periods of unified as well as divided government.

The consequences of the nation meeting or exceeding the legal debt limit help to explain the largely nonpartisan and nonideological nature of debt limit politics in the past. The annual federal budget was approximately $3.45 trillion in fiscal year 2013, and national defense claimed nearly 18 percent of spending while roughly 48 percent was dedicated to three entitlement programs: Social Security, Medicare, and Medicaid. An entitlement program is a program that sets criteria for eligibility and anyone fitting the criteria is *entitled* to receive its benefits. Unlike other items in the federal budget, entitlement programs are automatically funded. The only way to alter spending is through a change in the eligibility criteria or the promised benefits. Total federal revenue (mostly via taxes) was $2.8 trillion, with nearly 60 percent coming from individual income and corporate taxes. The difference between spending and revenue, or deficit, totaled $680 billion in 2013. The national debt was $16.7 trillion, an amount equal to the total value of the U.S. economy or gross domestic product (GDP) (Klimasinska 2013). Projected deficits were predicted to add another $6.3 trillion to total U.S. debt by 2023 (Congressional Budget Office 2013). As the name implies, debt limits restrict the Treasury Department's ability to respond to revenue shortfalls.

A 2013 report from the Congressional Research Service spells out what happens if the Treasury Department is hamstrung by a debt limit. A failure to pay the federal government's obligations could undermine the credit worthiness of the United States. As a result, the federal government may no longer be able to borrow money at lower interest rates. At present, the federal government is able to borrow money on very advantageous terms as it is seen as a safe investment with very little risk. When the federal government borrows money, it does it a bit differently than people or other institutions. The federal government "issues debt" by selling Treasury bills, notes, and bonds. People, businesses, and even governments and governmental agencies purchase this debt. The federal government then pays it back with interest. Often, the federal government will pay off existing debt by issuing new debt; not unlike a college student transferring the balance from a higher-interest-rate credit card to a new lower-interest-rate credit card. If the government was unable to make its payments, or defaulted, on its debt, it would no longer be seen as a safe investment. As a result, investors would demand better terms before buying Treasury bills or bonds. The federal government would respond by offering higher interest rates. This encourages investors to buy debt, but increases the cost to government when paying off the debt (Austin and Levit 2013).

Given the considerable consequences, the U.S. Congress has never failed to increase the debt limit and the federal government has never defaulted on its obligations. With few exceptions, debt limit politics was beyond the reach of ideological divisions. But in recent years, it has come close. The 2010 midterm elections saw the return of divided government in the United States as Republicans reclaimed the U.S. House of Representatives while Democrats retained control of the Senate and the presidency. Among the dozens of newly elected Republican members of Congress were a sizable faction of ideologically motivated fiscal conservatives elected as a result of the so-called Tea Party movement that emerged in the summer of 2009. Tea Partiers, as members of the movement are called, were mostly frustrated current or former Republicans who believed that the party had abandoned its fiscally conservative ideology. Tea Party candidates promised to impose strict spending discipline on Congress. The first evidence of this ideological commitment became clear early in 2011 after the swearing in of the new Congress.

In early March 2011, a vote was scheduled in the House to approve temporary spending measures in order to keep the federal government from shutting down. But the United States was fast approaching the statutory debt limit, so any spending measure would necessitate an increase in the debt ceiling. As retold by Stan Collender, a former staffer on both the House and

Senate budget committees, Tea Party leaders warned Republican members of Congress against voting in favor of any legislation that would increase the debt ceiling (Klein 2011). Many of the newly elected Republicans believed they had been sent to Washington to cut spending and there were no compromises to be made. The legislation to raise the debt ceiling was defeated in the House in early March.

In May of 2011, the U.S. Treasury Secretary announced that the United States had reached the legal debt limit and would exhaust all means by which to borrow money or cover debt by August 2 (Austin and Levit 2013). What followed was a two-year battle over the federal budget that pitted congressional Republicans against congressional Democrats and the White House. Key points of contention in the battle came down to longstanding ideological differences between conservatives and liberals regarding taxation and government spending on entitlement programs such as Medicare, Medicaid, and Social Security. Attempts to reach a compromise agreement revealed the deep ideological divisions present in Congress and the impact of those division on once-common institutional features.

Compromise in a Polarized Congress

Conservative Republicans in the House and Senate attempted to use the debt limit situation to force concessions from the Democratic Senate and president. A bill to increase the debt limit, with no strings attached, was soundly defeated in the House in late May 2011. On July 19, roughly two weeks before the August 2 deadline, the House passed the Cut, Cap, and Balance Act of 2011 (HR 2560). The bill contained several provisions popular among conservative members and voters. In exchange for an increase in the debt ceiling, the bill required over $100 billion in cuts to current-year spending and significant reductions in future spending (Congress 2011). The bill passed in the House by a near party-line vote. The bill was then sent to the Democratically-controlled Senate where it was tabled (put aside and ignored) (Wong 2011). It was never expected that the legislation would, but conservatives saw the passage in the House, coupled with the president's veto threat and defeat at the hands of Senate Democrats, as a symbolic victory that highlighted the ideological differences between the parties.

As the August 2 deadline approached and Congress debated measures to raise the debt limit, President Obama and Speaker Boehner began negotiations on a so-called Grand Bargain that would deal with long-standing budget challenges. Typically in the contemporary Congress, party leaders in the House hold significant power, but the influx of Tea Party Republicans in the 2010 midterm introduced uncertainty to the traditional power structure. Boehner only revealed his negotiations with Obama to a select few on his staff. It was in President Obama's best interests to keep the negotiations secret as well. Many on the Democratic left, including members of Congress, believed the president was too willing to compromise on issues that many Democrats considered to be sacred, such as spending on entitlement programs. So both leaders faced the very real possibility of open revolt among party members if news leaked too early regarding their negotiations (Bai 2012).

It is commonly accepted by nonpartisan analysts and experts that the only realistic way to deal with the nation's long-term debt and deficit problems is a two-pronged approach that both reduces future spending and increases future revenue. The necessity of the two-pronged solution also explains why the problem remains unaddressed. Congressional Republicans, especially Tea Party members, and conservative Republican Party activists oppose tax increases. They believe that tax increases take money out of the hands of consumers, stifle economic growth, and empower government. They contend as well that federal deficits are driven not by a lack of revenue but rather too much spending, especially on entitlement programs. Congressional Democrats and liberal party activists believe that entitlement programs are essential to economic growth and fairness and that budget deficits can best be addressed via reductions in other large budget items like defense spending and via higher taxes on upper-income individuals and corporations. Both sides view one prong of the two-pronged approach as anathema to their ideological beliefs. President Obama and Speaker Boehner understood that each must give in on areas unpopular within their parties. Boehner needed to accept new tax revenue and Obama needed to accept reductions in entitlement spending.

But both men believed that a grand bargain would be easier to sell in Congress than any of the smaller fixes that had proven so difficult. A grand bargain would require sacrifice on the part of liberal and conservatives. Neither side would be able to claim victory nor would either need to admit defeat. Though members may fear the backlash of party activists, they would be able to defend their unpopular votes by pointing to the long-term benefits of deficit reduction. In the end, Boehner agreed to an increase in revenue of approximately $800 billion over ten years—an amount equal to what would be raised were the Bush-era tax cuts for upper-income Americans allowed to expire. President Obama agreed to $1.4 trillion in cuts to discretionary spending (everything other than Medicare, Medicaid, and Social Security) over ten years. The two sides were nearing agreement on $360 billion in cuts to Medicare and Medicaid and unspecified savings for Social Security by altering the methodology used to calculate annual cost-of-living increases.

As word of the secret negotiations leaked, the reactions were as expected. Conservative Republicans balked at the idea of new revenue from taxes, hardly surprising given the growing influence of insurgent Tea Party conservatives in Congress. But ideological revolt went beyond Republicans and the Tea Party caucus. In the midst of the back and forth between the White House and Speaker Boehner, Democratic Minority Leader Nancy Pelosi and Minority Whip Hoyer, the two top leaders of the party in the House, rejected any calls for entitlement cuts, even if part of a grand bargain, declaring such cuts to be "off the table" (Beutler 2011).

Faced with the prospect of open ideological revolt, the attempts to reach a grand bargain quickly unraveled even as Obama and Boehner sought ways to keep their fellow partisans in line. To appease liberals, Obama proposed a new minimum of $1.16 trillion in additional revenue and a trigger mechanism that would automatically increase taxes on upper-income earners if Congress failed to enact legislation aimed at generating the new revenue. Attempts were made to appease conservatives by promising automatic cuts to entitlements and Boehner demanded the elimination of the individual mandate at the heart of the Affordable Care Act, a move that had little to do with deficit reduction but was a key policy goal of Tea Party members. Of course neither the president nor Democratic members of Congress would ever agree to eliminate the individual mandate, much as Republicans were unlikely ever to agree to automatic tax increases. With congressional Democrats and Republicans so divided, nearly any policy proposal offered to ensure the support of one side would become a deal breaker for the other side. With so few members occupying the political center, there is quite literally no common ground to be found, certainly no common ground sufficient to accommodate any grand budget agreements.

The negotiations between Boehner and Obama collapsed with only days remaining until the United States reached its legal debt limit. Congress responded by passing another temporary measure, the Budget Control Act of 2011. In exchange for a $900 billion increase to the debt limit, the legislation specified $917 billion in nonentitlement spending cuts over the following ten years. But the most unique element contained in the legislation was the creation of the Joint Select Committee on Deficit Reduction—quickly redubbed the Deficit Reduction Supercommittee (Dwyer and Miller 2011). It was tasked with producing legislation by Thanksgiving Day 2011, that would reduce the deficit by $1.5 trillion over ten years. Any legislation ultimately approved by the Supercommittee would be guaranteed an up or down vote in the House and Senate. No amendments would be allowed, no filibuster, and the president agreed to not veto the measure if passed by Congress.

The Supercommittee's twelve members were selected by the Republican and Democratic Party leaders in the House and the Senate—three members selected by each party leader in each chamber. As an incentive to motivate members to reach a deal, the legislation creating the Supercommittee contained a failsafe trigger. If the Supercommittee failed to reach an agreement or Congress failed to pass an agreement, then Congress would raise the debt limit by another $1.2 trillion and up to $1.2 trillion in automatic cuts to discretionary and entitlement spending would take effect beginning January of 2013. It was assumed that the threat of $1.2 trillion in mostly indiscriminate cuts to Republican-favored areas such as defense and Democratic-favored areas such as entitlements would be sufficient to overcome the ideological gridlock that had blocked prior deals.

The Democratic committee members proposed $3 trillion in deficit reduction, including $1.3 trillion in new revenue through taxes and approximately $400 billion in savings from Medicare. Republican members rejected the offer owing to the size of the tax increases and countered with a proposal for $1.2 trillion in deficit reduction with $300 billion in new revenue generated by lowering tax rates but closing existing tax loopholes that allowed some to avoid paying taxes. Democrats rejected the proposal owing to the proposed reduction in tax rates. After months of negotiations, the Supercommittee failed to reach an agreement (Dodge and Hunter 2011). Described as a triumph of ideology over compromise, each side quickly blamed ideological intransigence for the failure. Democratic senator John Kerry, a member of the Supercommittee, said the failure "underscores the rigidity and unwillingness of forces outside of Congress to allow for rational consensus" (Dodge and Hunter 2011). Kerry was referring to the ideological activists so crucial for fund-raising and for winning primaries.

The failure of the Supercommittee offers tremendous insight into the impact of deeply held ideological beliefs held by two opposing parties in an institution that requires consensus to function. Substantial bipartisan majorities were once responsible for the passage of significant legislation such as the creation of the Medicare and Medicaid program in 1965. But as noted by congressional scholar Sarah Binder in her book, *Stalemate: Causes and Consequences of Legislative Gridlock*, Congress is more likely to reach agreement on substantial issues when it is populated by moderate legislators divided among two centrist parties as it was at midcentury (Figure 5.3). However, as more members moved away from the political center and the parties began to polarize along ideological lines, gridlock and stalemate became more common (Binder 2003). The authors of "Toward a More Responsible Two-Party System" never really considered the difficulty two responsible and distinct parties may have reaching compromise in an era when divided party control of government is the norm. The Democratic and Republican membership of the Supercommittee mirrored the ideological distribution of their respective parties in Congress. No member neared the political center and the distance between the most moderate Democrat and the most moderate Republican was considerable. The Supercommittee was created due to the failure of party leaders to reach an overall budget agreement, so it is not surprising that a committee of members selected by party leadership also was unable to succeed.

Prospects for Change

The factors that contribute to ideological polarization show no indication of waning. Though some states have reformed their congressional redistricting process to favor a nonpartisan approach, most states continue to engage in a partisan process. Open primaries, in which any voter can participate in a party primary regardless of affiliation, are not the norm and many partisans oppose opening their nominating process to nonparty members. Even in states with open primaries, turnout is still dominated by more ideologically extreme candidates. This was witnessed in Virginia in the 2014 primary elections when Conservative Republican House Majority Leader Eric Cantor was defeated by a little-known insurgent candidate who accused Cantor of being too beholden to the Republican Party establishment. Virginia has non-partisan primaries, but this did not protect Cantor—already a conservative stalwart—from being challenged from his right flank.

Recent Supreme Court decisions striking down limits on corporate campaign contributions and on an individual's aggregate campaign contributions are likely to contribute to ever-more expensive campaigns and the need by candidates to raise ever-more money (Sullivan 2014). By most accounts, the 2014 midterm election was the most expensive midterm election in history with an estimated $3.4 billion spent by the parties, candidates, and outside organizations and groups (Tafani 2014). Based on current research, more money should translate into more ideological candidates (Heberlig, Hetherington, and Larson 2006).

As gatekeepers of the agenda and redistributors of campaign cash, party leaders are expected to promote the best electoral interests of their party. This often means finding ways to motivate party voters. One effective way to motivate those voters is the creation of so-called wedge issues that heighten awareness of the divide between the two parties and the possible consequences of electoral defeat. This "creates incentives for the leaders of the two parties to transform potentially nonpartisan matters, such as budget process reform" or other seemingly benign issues into divisive, party line issues" (Evans 2012, 81). The desire to highlight party differences as a means to motivate partisan voters encourages a situation in which there is little distinction between legislating and campaigning.

Republicans regained unified control of Congress following the midterm elections of 2014. In a testament to the power of fund-raising, Democratic Minority Leader Nancy Pelosi was reelected to that post following the 2014 midterms even as she led Democratic House members through their third consecutive election loss. Perhaps Pelosi's greatest claim to the position was that she has raised over $400 million for congressional Democrats since assuming a leadership position in 2002. Liberal party activists like Nancy Pelosi and express it via their checkbooks.

Though unified party control of the House and Senate may remove some impediments to compromise between the two chambers, the Democratic minority in the Senate retains the ability to filibuster Republican legislation and President Obama has the authority to veto any legislation with which he disagrees. Though Republicans enjoy their largest House majority in over sixty years, they still have too few voters in either the House or the Senate to overcome a veto. Ideological polarization is likely to remain a hallmark of the modern Congress for many years to come.

References

Aldrich, J., and D. Rohde. 2009. "Congressional Committees in a Continuing Partisan Era." In L. Dodd, and D. Oppenheimer, *Congress Reconsidered*, 217–40. Washington, DC: CQ Press.

APSA. 1950. "Toward a More Responsible Two-Party System: A Report of the Committee on Political Parties." *American Political Science Research* 44 (3): 99.

Austin, A., and M. Levit. 2013. *The Debt Limit: History and Recent Increases.* Washington, DC: Congressional Research Service.

Bafumi, J., and M. Herron. 2009. "Leapfrog Representation and Extremism: A Study of American Voters and Their Members of Congress." *American Political Science Review* 104 (3): 519–42.

Bai, M. 2012. "Obama vs. Boehner: Who Killed the Debt Deal?" *New York Times.* March 28. http://www.nytimes.com/2012/04/01/magazine/obama-vs-boehner-who-killed-the-debt-deal.html?pagewanted=all (accessed August 4, 2014).

Beutler, B. 2011. "Hoyer: Dems United Against Entitlement Benefit Cuts in Debt Fight. Talking Points Memo." July 19. http://talkingpointsmemo.com/dc/hoyer-dems-united-against-entitlement-benefit-cuts-in-debt-fight (accessed August 26, 2014).

Binder, S. 2003. *Stalemate: Causes and Consequences of Legislative Gridlock.* Washington, DC: Brookings Institution Press.

Brady, D., H. Han, and J. Pope. 2007. "Primary Elections and Candidate Ideology: Out of Step with the Primary Electorate?" *Legislative Studies Quarterly* 32 (1): 79–105.

Coffey, D. 2011. "More than a Dime's Worth: Using State Party Platforms to Assess the Degree of American Party Polarization." *PS: Political Science and Politics* 44 (2): 331–37.

Congress, T. L. 2011. *Bill Summary and Status 112th Congress (2011 - 2012) H.R. 2560.* THOMAS. July 22. http://thomas.loc.gov/cgi-bin/bdquery/z?d112:h.r.2560 (accessed August 5, 2014).

Congressional Budget Office. 2013. *Updated Budget Projections: Fiscal Years 2013 to 2023.* Congressional Budget Office. May 14. http://www.cbo.gov/publication/44172 (accessed August 5, 2014).

Cox, G., and Matthew McCubbins. 1993. *Legislative Leviathan: Party Government in the House.* Berkeley: University of California Press.

Dodge, C., and K. Hunter. 2011. "U.S. Supercommittee Fails to Reach Agreement as Across-the-Board Cuts Loom." Bloomburg. November 21. http://www.bloomberg .com/news/2011-11-21/supercommittee-fails-to-reach-agreement-on-1-2-trillion-deficit-reduction.html (accessed August 26, 2014).

Dwyer, D., and S. Miller. 2011. "Debt-Ceiling Deal: President Obama Signs Bill as Next Fight Looms." ABC News. August 2. http://abcnews.go.com/Politics/debt-ceiling-deal-president-obama-signs-bill-fight-looms/story?id=14213050 (accessed August 26, 2014).

Evans, C. L. 2012. "Parties and Leaders: Polarization and Power in the U.S. House and Senate." In J. L. Carson, *New Directions in Congressional Politics,* 65–84. New York: Routledge.

Fiorina, M., and S. Abrams. 2009. *Disconnect: The Breakdown of Representation in American Politics.* Norman: University of Oklahoma Press.

Heberlig, E., M. Hetherington, and B. Larson. 2006. "The Price of Leadership: Campaign Money and the Polarization of Congressional Parties." *The Journal of Politics* 68 (4): 992–1005.

Jacobson, G. 2012. "The Electoral Origins of Polarized Politics: Evidence from the 2010 Cooperative Congressional Election Study." *American Behavioral Scientist* 56 (12): 1612–30.

Klein, E. 2011. "The Tea Party and the Debt Ceiling." *Washington Post.* July 14. http:// www.washingtonpost.com/blogs/wonkblog/post/the-tea-party-and-the-debt-ceiling/2011/07/11/gIQAHaldEI_blog.html (accessed August 5, 2014).

Klimasinska, K. 2013. "Budget Deficit in U.S. Narrows to 5-Year Low on Record Revenue." Bloomberg. October 30. http://www.bloomberg.com/news/2013-10-30/budget-deficit-in-u-s-narrows-to-5-year-low-on-record-revenue.html (accessed August 5, 2014).

Murray, S., and L. Montgomery. 2010. "Angry Democrats Rebel against Obama's Tax-Cut Deal with Republicans." *Washington Post.* December 8. http://www .washingtonpost.com/wp-dyn/content/article/2010/12/07/AR2010120707230.html (accessed August 5, 2014).

Putnam, R. 2001. *Bowling Alone: The Collapse and Revival of American Community.* New York: Simon & Schuster.

Schier, S., and T. Eberly. 2013. *American Government and Popular Discontent: Stability without Success.* New York: Routledge.

Sinclair, B. 2012. *Unorthodox Lawmaking*, 4th ed. Los Angeles: Sage.

Sullivan, S. 2014. "Everything You Need to Know about *McCutcheon v. FEC.*" *Washington Post*. April 2. http://www.washingtonpost.com/blogs/the-fix/wp/2013/10/08/supreme-court-takes-up-the-sequel-to-citizens-united/ (accessed August 28, 2014).

Thompsen, D. 2014. "Ideological Moderates Won't Run: How Party Fit Matters for Partisan Polarization in Congress." *The Journal of Politics* 76 (3): 786–97.

Wong, S. 2011. "Senate Rejects 'Cut, Cap and Balance.'" *Politico*. July 22. http://www.politico.com/news/stories/0711/59661.html (accessed August 4, 2014).

6

Ideology in the Federal and State Courts

IN RECENT DECADES, FEDERAL AND STATE COURTS have given judges' ideology a greater role in their decisions. Policymaking is now a major function of many courts. Such court behavior got its start through a revolution in the federal judiciary's role beginning in 1954 and consummated during the 1960s and 1970s. In 1984, political scientist Herbert Jacob defined the then-new trend away from traditional norm enforcement and toward judicial policymaking: "The difference lies in the intended impact of the decision. Policy decisions are intended to be guideposts for future actions; norm enforcement decisions are aimed at the particular case at hand" (Jacob 1984, 37). In making policy, judges bring their personal ideology to bear upon their court decisions.

The impetus for expanded policymaking came from the Supreme Court, specifically the court headed by Chief Justice Earl Warren from 1954 to 1968. In a series of sweeping decisions, the Warren Court created national policy regarding racial integration, state and local criminal justice, conditions in state and local prisons, school prayer, the personal right to privacy, and state and federal legislative apportionment. In these decisions, the Warren court set ideologically liberal guideposts for a big variety of federal, state, and local government actions.

Intense ideological disputes erupted over these findings, resulting in incensed responses such as billboards urging "Impeach Earl Warren." Accompanying the audacious policymaking of the Supreme Court were changes in legal rules and federal court practices during the 1960s and 1970s that made policymaking much more common by federal judges—institutionalizing the practice. Many state courts have followed the federal courts' policymaking lead.

Congress, for its part, abetted federal judicial policymaking by passing many new liberal domestic laws in the 1960s and 1970s that permitted adjudication as a means of enforcement (Farhang 2010). The number of judicial branch personnel grew considerably as well. Presidents, consumed by their duties, conceded the importance of judicial policymaking by emphasizing ideological considerations in federal judicial appointments. Liberals and many Democrats favored judges who endorsed a "living constitution" that would accommodate new governmental initiatives and create new rights for citizens. Conservatives and most Republicans endorsed judges favoring a more "strict construction" of the Constitution that would be wary of new governmental programs and the creation of new rights. Led by Supreme Court Justice Antonin Scalia, many judicial conservatives in recent decades assert that federal court decisions should conform to the "original intent" of the authors of the Constitution.

Judicial appointment politics gradually became subject to the partisan and ideological polarization in the U.S. Senate. New judicial policymaking avenues spurred the creation and activity of ideological interest groups. In the 1960s, a "liberal legal network" formed to vigorously pursue policy change through the courts. This produced a countermobilization of think tanks and interest groups promoting a conservative judicial agenda (Teles 2008, 22–90). Since the 1960s, interest groups, congressional and judicial personnel, and the number of federal regulations all increased apace. The impact upon America's national political system was great, creating a complex, elite arena of policymaking dominated by legal professionals and interest groups.

A major result was "the judicialization of politics—the reliance of courts and judicial means for addressing core moral predicaments, public policy questions, and political controversies . . . arguably one of the most significant phenomena of late twentieth and early twenty-first century government" (Hirschl 2008, 119). Judicial policymaking is a central aspect of the rising importance of ideology in American governance. Judicial politics involves complex battles by political elites. Its guiding forces are many federal judges and state judges. All federal judges receive lifetime appointments and rarely are removed from office. Popular accountability is largely lacking from this federal policymaking arena, except through the indirect mechanism of presidential and senatorial elections. Twelve states never subject the judges of their highest courts to reelection. The thirty-nine states that subject at least some judges from high, appellate, or district courts to the voters seldom have jurists removed from office at the polls.

The Origins of Judicial Policymaking

The public never voted to make judges "legislators in robes" and until the 1960s and 1970s, the courts rarely operated as such. It may not seem obvious that changes in America's party system helped to create judicial policymaking, but that is the case. As the New Deal party system crumbled in the 1960s, parties themselves became dominated by issue activists sharing common ideological agendas. Unlike the old-style pragmatic party leaders they replaced, these activists sought to put their ideological stamp on the judiciary and formed liberal and conservative interest groups to pursue that end. In the late 1960s, political scientist Nancy Scherer notes, the demands of ideologically driven party activists and issue group leaders led to federal judicial appointments on ideological grounds, partisan polarization in the appointment process, and big differences in judicial behavior by judges depending upon which party dominated the appointment process at the time of their appointment (Scherer 2005, 38–45). Political scientist Robert Kagan notes that as parties weakened it made sense for "interest groups and momentarily strong political coalitions to demand enactment of highly detailed laws, enforceable in court" to help "insulate today's policy victories from reversal following tomorrow's electoral loss" (Kagan 2001, 49). Congress and many state legislatures in the 1960s and 1970s obliged.

For most of American constitutional history before the 1960s, the courts functioned differently and so did the judicial appointment process. Courts before then were "small in number and, with only occasional exceptions, small in their impact on public policy" (Mackenzie 1996, 135). Judicial appointments operated on the basis of patronage, not ideology: "Because the old party system left judicial selection in the hands of local party leaders and home state senators who placed their patrons on the bench, the appointees of a given president—Democrat or Republican—were ideologically heterogeneous, just a local party leaders and home state senators were ideologically heterogeneous" (Scherer 2005, 28–29). Because courts seldom made policy but confined themselves to norm enforcement in particular controversies, few interest groups paid attention to judicial selection. Most lawyers were sole practitioners in contrast to the "mega law firms" of today. Congress and state legislatures took less initiative in domestic policy, producing fewer legal controversies for the courts to address.

Now, courts are far more likely to approve legislative expansions of government policy, and where courts have deemed legislative action was insufficient, courts have made policy themselves: "setting standards, issuing detailed rules, establishing goals—generally performing a broad array of what had once been conceived of solely as legislative or administrative responsibilities"

(Mackenzie 1996, 134). Beginning with the Warren Court, such policymaking gradually became institutionalized as a normal practice of the federal and state judiciary. That allowed judges' personal ideology to have a much bigger impact on court decisions.

Institutionalizing Judicial Policymaking

The institutionalization of judicial policymaking occurred gradually, in several steps from the 1950s to the 1980s. The U.S. Supreme Court inaugurated the process with its landmark decisions *Brown v. Board of Education of Topeka* 347 U.S. 483 (1954) and 349 U.S. 294 (1955). In the first decision, the court ruled that segregation of public schools by law (de jure segregation) was a violation of the Fourteenth Amendment's requirement that no state may deny its citizens "equal protection of the laws." In justifying its decision, the court relied on the findings of recent social science, arguing that segregation marks the "colored race" with a "badge of inferiority." The policy action produced a sweeping restructuring of race relations. It is arguably one of the most important liberal policy decisions of the twentieth century. The second *Brown* decision began a new process of "structural remedies" to enforce policies announced by the court, in this case in the original 1954 decision. In *Brown II*, the court ordered affected districts to desegregate with "all deliberate speed" and required federal district courts to oversee the desegregation process. With the cooperation of the Department of Justice, this administrative regime slowly rolled back legal segregation in state and local school districts.

Judicial scholar Gordon Silverstein explains how the *Brown* decisions boosted judicial policymaking: "[W]hen the Warren Court first signaled the possibility that, in addition to its traditional function of saying what government *could* and what it could *not* do, the courts might now also be available to say what government *must* do as well, the Justices opened a new path to policy goals" (Silverstein 2009, 29).

So it proved. Since the *Brown* decisions, federal courts have ordered structural remedies to pursue liberal goals in several policy areas. The Supreme Court in *Swann v. Charlotte Mecklenburg Board of Education* 42 U.S. 1 (1971) issued an extensive list of structural remedies, including mandatory busing, to remedy legally segregated schools. Federal District Judge Arthur Garrity in the 1970s single-handedly supervised the desegregation of Boston schools by requiring busing and supervising the implementation of busing plans. Federal courts applied the Eighth Amendment's ban on "cruel and unusual punishments" in regulating state prison systems and requiring several state legislatures to fund prison improvements (Feeley and Rubin, 2000). Federal

Judge Frank M. Johnson Jr. in 1972 handed down rulings that established minimum standards for providing treatment in state mental health facilities in Alabama that he deemed inadequate. From 1972 to 2003, when federal court supervision concluded, implementation of these standards reshaped the mental health system in Alabama and in the nation (Ziegler 2003).

Lawsuits became a prime vehicle for making policy through courts. At the federal level, the Supreme Court in 1966 amended the Federal Rule of Civil Procedure 24a, relaxing the rules for interveners to have "standing to sue" in federal cases, opening the way for an avalanche of lawsuits in federal courts in ensuing decades. From 1950 to 1969, the number of civil lawsuits involving the U.S. government as a plaintiff or defendant stood at about 22,500 per year. In the 1970s, that civil caseload doubled and by 1985 it had doubled again (Dungworth and Pace 1990, 8). During that time, federal courts began to respond favorably to "class action" lawsuits filed on behalf of large groups of people, not individual litigants, regarding product liability, medical malpractice, environmental protection, and the government's use of "eminent domain" to seize privately owned lands (Lieberman 1981, 41, 67, 103, 149). Courts in the 1960s and 1970s gained the ability to make rules regarding large groups of citizens through lawsuits. The broader grounds for lawsuits are still largely in place today, as are much larger numbers of civil suits involving the national government than before 1970 (Administrative Office of the U.S. Courts 2012, Table C-2A). Many states adopted rules similar to the new federal procedures, producing an increase in class action lawsuits in state courts.

Congress abetted the institutionalization of judicial policymaking by passing many liberal social and environmental laws. Between 1964 and 1977, Congress passed twenty-five major civil rights and environmental acts, plus new legal regulations regarding workplace safety, consumer lending, product safety, private pension funds, and local public education. Included among these were the Civil Rights Act (1964), National Traffic and Motor Safety Act (1966), National Environmental Protection Act (1972), the Clean Air Act (1970), the Occupational Safety and Health Act (1970), the Clean Water Act (1972), and the Equal Employment Opportunity Act (1972). The laws expanded bureaucratic regulations, which were then adjudicated in the courts.

Judicial scholar Robert Kagan explains how many of these laws greatly increased litigation and spawned more judicial policymaking: "Congress assigned primary enforcement responsibility to state and local government officials. But then how could reformers and their Congressional allies be sure that the new federal norms would be faithfully implemented? . . . individual victims of injustice and energetic reform lawyers could act as 'private attorneys general',' bringing lawsuits against state and local governments for half-hearted implementation of federal laws, or they could sue regulated businesses directly" (Kagan 2001, 47). Congress, in other words, came "to rely on private litigation in statutory implementation" (Farhang 2010, 3). National legislators avoided the at times messy politics of implementation and left them to the courts. That gave the courts the ability to define implementation, that is, to make policy.

The Supreme Court, for its part, after 1954 became less deferential toward Congress and the president. Federal judges are now far less likely to have had legislative or executive experience than those on the court decades ago. None of the present members of the Supreme Court, for example, have such backgrounds. With less experience in other realms of governance, the Supreme Court in recent decades has more vigorously stamped its interpretation upon Congress and presidential actions. From 1789 to 1960, the Supreme Court declared seventy-two federal laws and 689 state and local laws unconstitutional. Since 1960, the court had ruled eighty-nine federal laws and 612 state and local laws unconstitutional, a much brisker pace. Constitutional interpretation is a fundamental form of national policymaking, a major duty the Supreme Court in recent decades aggressively has pursued.

All this adds up to a federal judiciary in which "litigation is more like problem solving than grievance-answering" (Horowitz 1977, 7). Kagan described federal judicial policymaking as an enduring regime of "adversarial legalism" whose basic structures are: "the fragmentation of governmental and regulatory authority among levels of government and many agencies; a dense web of highly prescriptive, analytically and procedurally demanding statutes; and ready access by affected interests to a politically selected, self-confident and rather unpredictable judiciary" (Kagan 2001, 232). Such a regime is "very easy to maintain and very difficult to dislodge" (Teles 2008, 14). It provides an arena for ideological conflict between two groups of federal judges: liberals appointed by Democratic presidents who support a "living constitution" and conservative advocates of "strict construction" and "originalism" appointed by GOP presidents.

Ideology in Supreme Court Decision Making

Political scientists have long known that ideology drives much decision making by justices on the U.S. Supreme Court as well as judges on the thirteen U.S. Circuit Courts of Appeal and ninety-four Federal District Courts. Many studies of Supreme Court decisions demonstrate a great linkage between justice's ideology and their votes on cases before the court. One examination of court decisions from 1953 to 1999 found a high correlation between a justice's values, measured by descriptions of them in newspaper editorials at the time of their nomination, and their subsequent votes while on the Supreme Court. That study also found that judges' ideology had a stronger impact on their court decisions than did the facts of the case before them (Segal and Spaeth 2002, 321–25).

The current Supreme Court divides closely between ideological conservatives and liberals. Chief Justice John Roberts and Justices Antonin Scalia, Clarence Thomas, and Samuel Alito—all appointed by GOP presidents—are usually reliable conservative votes, often favoring "strict construction" and "originalism." Justices Ruth Bader Ginsberg, Stephen Breyer, Elena Kagan, and Sonia Sotomayor—appointed by Democratic presidents—are liberals more sympathetic to the concept of a "living constitution." Justice Anthony Kennedy, appointed by Ronald Reagan, is a less-reliable conservative vote and at times provided the deciding "swing vote" in important cases. Table 6.1 shows three sets of ideology scores for the current justices. Though differing in method, all three show two factions: four conservative justices (with high scores on each of the scales) and four liberal justices (with lower scores) and Justice Kennedy in the middle but closer to the conservative block.

The liberal–conservative ideological divide also is prominent in federal circuit courts, the appellate courts between federal district courts and the Supreme Court. A study of federal circuit court judges discovered strong

TABLE 6.1
Ideological Voting of Current Supreme Court Justices

Segal-Cover Score	*Martin-Quinn Score*	*Epstein et al. Score*
Conservatives (score and rank most conservative)		
Scalia 1.00 (1st)	Thomas 3.84 (1st)	Thomas 0.87 (2nd)
Alito 0.90 (3rd)	Scalia 2.73 (3rd)	Alito 0.82 (4th)
Roberts 0.88 (6th)	Alito 1.77 (8th)	Scalia 0.81 (5th)
Thomas 0.84 (7th)	Roberts 1.70 (9th)	Roberts 0.72 (11th)
Swing (score and rank most conservative)		
Kennedy 0.64 (14th)	Kennedy 0.83 (18th)	Kennedy 0.69 (15th)
Liberal (score and rank most conservative)		
Ginsberg 0.32 (21st)	Ginsberg -1.16 (34th)	Ginsberg 0.23 (36th)
Sotomayor 0.22 (29th)	Sotomayor -0.23 (29th)	Sotomayor 0.25 (33rd)
Breyer 0.52 (16th)	Breyer -1.01 (33rd)	Breyer 0.31 (30th)
Kagan 0.27 (24th)		

Listed by score and rank as most conservative justice among all justices serving from 1937. Higher scores indicate more conservative voting.
Source: Lee Epstein, William M. Landes, and Richard A. Posner, *The Behavior of Federal Judges: A Theoretical and Empirical Study of Rational Choice* (Cambridge, MA: Harvard University Press, 2013), 111.
Justice Kagan's score is from Jeffrey A. Segal, "Perceived Qualifications and Ideology of Supreme Court Nominees, 1937–2012," http://www.stonybrook.edu/commcms/polisci/jsegal/QualTable.pdf. (accessed November 21, 2013).

patterns of ideological voting—Democratically-appointed liberals and GOP-appointed conservatives—on controversial cases involving abortion, capital punishment, and gay and lesbian rights (Sunstein et al. 2006). A comprehensive examination of federal judicial decision making revealed that "ideology influences judicial decisions at all levels of the federal judiciary" but that "it diminishes as one moves down the judicial hierarchy" (Epstein, Landes, and Posner 2013, 385).

Ideological decision making is less evident among lower federal and state courts. Why? Lower courts are more likely to follow precedents of decisions made previously by higher courts in the federal court system or court system of their state. Lower courts have less control over the cases that come before them than do appellate courts. Furthermore, audacious policymaking by lower courts risks reversal from courts above them. That means lower courts deal more with cases requiring norm enforcement of established laws and are less inclined to seek out opportunities for sweeping policymaking.

The federal courts overall have been trending toward more Democratically-appointed and liberal judges thanks to appointments by President Obama. The number of conservatives and liberals on the federal bench became equal in 2013, with the circuit courts now having more liberal than conservative judges. By the end of the Obama presidency, the federal courts will have a majority of Democratically-appointed judges (Wolf 2013).

Policymaking and Ideology in State Supreme Courts

State supreme courts followed the Warren Court's lead into judicial policy-making. A survey of the role of state supreme courts concluded: "As courts of last resort, state supreme courts have the final authority on many issues that are critical to citizens' daily lives and to the overall nature of state politics and policy. Furthermore, state supreme courts exercise extraordinary discretion in rendering decisions" (Brace, Hall, and Langer 2001). With broad discretion comes the opportunity for judges to insert their personal ideology into court decisions. The state supreme courts' review of state laws is "the most activist form of judicial policymaking because judges are substituting their policy choices for those of coequal officials in the legislative branch of government" (Emmert and Traut 1992). Studies of the role of state supreme courts in state education and abortion policymaking found this to be the case (Wilhelm 2007; Brace, Hall, and Langer 2001).

An example of state supreme court policymaking with national impact involves the controversy over same-sex marriage. Legalization of same-sex marriage requires an innovative application of parts of state constitutions to same-sex couples, a transformation of a state's "living constitution" in accord with the socially liberal agenda favoring same-sex marriage. The first three states to legalize same-sex marriage—Massachusetts in 2003, California in 2008, and Iowa in 2009—did so through decisions by state supreme courts. In the 2008 California decision, differing ideologies were on display. Chief Justice George, in announcing the 4-3 opinion, announced a new legal doctrine and social policy: "the failure to designate the official relationship of same-sex couples as marriage violates . . . the California Constitution." Justice Baxter, in a partial dissent, objected to this instance of judicial policymaking and urged judicial restraint: "A bare majority of this court, not satisfied with the pace of democratic change . . . substitutes, by judicial fiat, its own social policy views for those expressed by the people themselves" (In re Marriage Cases 2008, 298, 457–58). The California decision led to 2008's Proposition 8, passed by the state's voters, banning same-sex marriage. A federal district court later ruled Proposition 8 unconstitutional and the U.S. Supreme Court upheld that ruling in *Hollingsworth v. Perry* 570 U.S. ___ (2013). From the momentum derived from the state high court decisions, legislatures in twelve other states approved gay marriage from 2009 to 2013. All twelve states had Democratic governors and legislatures. The U.S. Supreme Court in 2015 followed the state supreme courts' lead in a 5-4 decision establishing a constitutional right to same-sex marriage in *Obergefell v. Hodges* 576 U.S. _____ (2015).

Numerous studies have identified the varying ideological tendencies among the fifty state high courts. A 2012 analysis found that 171 state supreme court justices were liberal and 165 were conservative. The most liberal state supreme courts were those of New Mexico, Maine, Oregon, New Hampshire, and Washington. South Dakota, Texas, North Dakota, Alabama, and Idaho had he most conservative state supreme courts (Judgepedia 2013). The ideological divisions evident in state and federal courts also exist in America's legal profession. A reconfigured legal profession, riven by ideological divisions yet committed to pursuing policy solutions in court, provides a vital support structure for contemporary judicial policymaking in the national and state courts.

Ideological Lawyers and Their Use of Courts

Accompanying the rise in liberal federal and state court activism was a huge growth in the number of American lawyers and of liberal legal crusades. The total number of American lawyers swelled from 180,000 in 1940 to almost 800,000 by 1988 (Mackenzie 1996, 136). Many law schools, busy producing a burgeoning population of lawyers, gave birth to a new "Liberal Legal Network" (Teles 2008, 22–58). Following the Warren Court's path-breaking decision

Gideon v. Wainwright 372 U.S. 365 in 1963, which established a "due process" civil right for indigent criminal defendants to be guaranteed a lawyer in criminal trials, many law schools developed programs in "public interest law." Law in the public interest directed legal efforts broadly toward social change, through such means as representation of criminal defendants and class action suits to achieve liberal policy ends. The Ford Foundation funded legal clinics in many leading law schools aimed at advocacy of legal services for the poor and for social change (Teles 2008, 38–41). Congress responded to President Johnson's request for a new federally funded Legal Services Program (LSP) to provide legal help to the poor. The previously conservative American Bar Association endorsed new liberal initiatives, becoming a strong advocate of the LSP. The LSP proved effective at liberal advocacy in federal courts. Between 1966 and 1974, the LSP submitted 169 cases to the Supreme Court and had 73 percent accepted for court action, a rate higher than the president's own solicitor general during that time (Lawrence 1990, Appendix C).

The Liberal Legal Network (LLN) developed into a dominant player in federal judicial policymaking just as the liberal Democratic governance of the mid-1960s was receiving a rebuke from voters at the ballot box in the 1966 and 1968 elections. Despite this, several factors allowed the LLN to entrench itself in judicial politics. Political scientist Steven Teles lists several reasons why the LLN was able to entrench itself. First, the legal profession—from law schools to the ABA—embraced new modes of liberal legal activism. Second, liberal legalism seemed a civilized alternative to violent protest erupting in the late 1960s. Third, the federal courts, with the Warren Court at the lead, and the federal government through the LSP created new resources and venues for liberal activism. Fourth, the rhetoric of "rights" gained great moral sway in the 1960s. Fifth, elite foundations, led by the Ford Foundation, funded a new "liberal legal support structure" in law schools and public-service law programs (Teles 2008, 56). In all, a powerful faction of legal professionals found the new avenues of federal judicial policymaking very suitable to the pursuit of liberal ends. Increasing the scale and complexity of judicial policymaking served the LLN's policy goals well. The concurrent rise in federal court lawsuits, cases in federal courts of appeals, and appeals to the Supreme Court has persisted since the rise of the LLN in the 1960s (Teles 2008, 265–74). State courts became important venues for the network to pursue its ideological goals as well.

The continued high level of LLN activity in federal and state courts generated a conservative response. Judicial policymaking became, in the decades since the 1960s, an enduring battlefield of polarized liberal and conservative legal elites. Conflicts over judicial policymaking continued in federal court but also spilled over into congressional appointment battles and electoral politics. The first filibuster against a Supreme Court nominee in American history came against Abe Fortas, a judicial liberal nominated by President Johnson in 1968. Richard Nixon during that year's presidential campaign pledged to appoint "law and order" judges who shared his judicial philosophy—one much more conservative that that evident in the Warren Court. Nixon pursued this by appointing the more conservative Warren Burger as Warren's successor as Chief Justice. The Democratic majority Senate rejected other conservative nominees to the court, Clement Haynsworth and G. Harold Carswell, the first time since 1894 that two consecutive Supreme Court nominees had been turned down.

The Burger Court, however, gradually earned a reputation as "the counterrevolution that wasn't" by producing large-scale, liberal policy change in three landmark decisions: *Swann v. Charlotte-Mecklenburg Board of Education* 402 U.S. 1 (1971), endorsing school busing as a structural remedy to de jure segregation; *Roe v. Wade* 410 U.S. 113 (1973), establishing a woman's abortion decision as part of a constitutionally protected right to privacy; and *University of California Davis v. Bakke* 438 U.S. 265 (1978), permitting race to be considered as a factor in college admissions as "affirmative action." Justice Harry Blackmun authored the *Roe* majority opinion and Justice Lewis Powell the *Bakke* majority opinion; both were Nixon appointees. Only Nixon's last appointee, William Rehnquist, proved to be a reliably conservative justice. His conservative fidelity gained him appointment as Chief Justice by Ronald Reagan in 1986 upon Berger's retirement.

While the Nixon administration attempted to stock the federal courts with more ideological conservatives, right-leaning legal professionals began organizing in ways to rival the LLN. In the 1970s, initial attempts to create conservative legal foundations funded by business proved of limited effectiveness because of their initial state-level focus and emphasis on parochial business concerns (Teles 2007, 75–78). The next major step in the brewing conservative counterrevolution came with the election of Ronald Reagan in 1980. Reagan's Justice Department made ideological screening of federal judicial candidates a top priority. The cumulative impact of Reagan and Nixon Supreme Court appointments became evident in the late 1980s, when the court moved in a more conservative direction.

Conservative "legal entrepreneurs" founded the Federalist Society in 1982, an organization that since that time has challenged legal liberalism in federal and state courts and provided a pipeline of conservative nominees for GOP presidents. Current Supreme Court Chief Justice John Roberts and Associate Justice Samuel Alito are members. On its website in 2012, the organization claims, "Law schools and the legal profession are currently strongly dominated by a form of orthodox liberal ideology" and that it "is founded on the principles that the state exists to preserve freedom, that the separation of governmental powers is central to our Constitution, and that it is emphatically the province and duty of the judiciary to say what the law is, not what it should be" (Federalist Society 2012).

Other interest groups formed in the 1970s and 1980s to enlist in ideological battle over the courts. Conservatives formed organizations such as Judicial Watch and the Institute of Justice; liberals countered with the Alliance for Justice, People for the American Way, and the National Organization for Women, alongside the longstanding liberal mainstay, the American Civil Liberties Union. One prime location of interest-group battles involved federal judicial appointments. The groups testified during nomination hearings, ran television ads against Supreme Court nominees, directly lobbied legislators, and filed briefs in court cases. Interviews with judicial-interest groups' leaders revealed a common belief on their part "that the federal courts wield significant power in implementing public policy" (Scherer 2005, 195). Beyond these core judicial groups, interest-group involvement in federal judicial appointment politics became vast. One study found that 448 groups expressed formal opinions about one or more federal judicial nominees in one two-year period, 1998–1999 (Bell 2002, 88).

Growing Conflict over Federal Court Appointments

Senate opponents of presidential nominees to federal district and appeals courts began during the Reagan presidency (Scherer 2005, 148–50). Democrats throughout the 1980s began to employ a variety of strategies to derail objectionable federal court nominees: inaction, delay, filibusters, and refusing to bargain with the White House. Confirmation conflicts, however, first erupted into total warfare surrounding the Reagan administration's nomination of Robert Bork to the Supreme Court in 1987. Bork previously served in Nixon's Justice Department as Solicitor General, the administration's chief lawyer, and was an outspoken opponent of liberal judicial policymaking. The Senate Judiciary Committee held widely televised hearings at which Bork himself discussed at length his judicial philosophy. Interest groups ran ads against Bork, asking citizens to call their senators to register their opinions on the matter; subsequently the phone lines were jammed. The Democratic-majority committee ultimately rejected Bork's nomination on a party-line vote. Reagan's next nominee, Anthony Kennedy, was a much less outspoken conservative and won Senate confirmation with less fanfare.

The Bork battle was tepid compared to the conflict over the nomination of black conservative Clarence Thomas to the court in 1991 by George Herbert Walker Bush. Bush's first appointment was the relatively obscure David Souter, who said little about his judicial philosophy during the appointment process and proved to be a far more liberal judicial policymaker on the bench than Bush had desired. Thomas, in contrast, was a well-known conservative figure. Interest groups on both ideological sides testified, ran ads, and urged public contact of lawmakers. Anita Hill, a former employee of Thomas's at the Equal Employment Opportunity Commission, charged Thomas with sexual harassment during public hearing. No conclusive proof of the charges ever surfaced, and Thomas was confirmed by a narrow 52–48 margin by a Senate controlled 56-44 by Democrats.

Bill Clinton's two nominees, Ruth Bader Ginsberg and Stephen Breyer, won confirmation from the Democratically-controlled Senate with little difficulty. After the GOP gained control of Congress in 1995, conflict over judicial appointments expanded to include several battles over federal district and appeals court nominees. GOP senators resorted to inaction, delay, filibusters, and refusing to bargain with the White House to stop unacceptable Clinton federal court nominees. Conflict within the Senate continued during George W. Bush's presidency, as lower federal court nominations faced unprecedented difficulties gaining Senate approval as the use of filibusters increased. At the time, sixty votes were required to end filibusters, effectively empowering the Democrats, the Senate minority party after 2002. By the spring of 2005, Democrats had successfully filibustered several nominees for federal appeals courts. GOP leaders in response proposed a number of ways to curtail the use of filibusters regarding judicial confirmations. Most dramatic was Senate Majority Leader Bill Frist's proposal, dubbed by Democrats the "nuclear option," in which a series of parliamentary rulings would declare filibusters against nominations unconstitutional. Democrats threatened to shut down the Senate completely in response, and Frist withdrew his proposal (Binder and Maltzman 2009, 100).

With the Democratic takeover of Congress in 2007, G. W. Bush's success in obtaining federal court confirmations fell to 77 percent, well below the 90 and above levels registered by Presidents Carter through Clinton. Barack Obama's first two years in office yielded a much lower success rate of 58 percent (Alliance for Justice 2011, 21). Confirmation wars by then had reached new levels of intensity in a Senate strongly polarized by two overlapping factors: ideology and partisanship. The advent of partisan and ideological media contributed to the bitter confirmation wars as website, cables news channels, and radio programs took sides and rallied the faithful liberals and conservatives in support or opposition of nominees.

In 2013, the Democratic majority finally exercised a "nuclear option" by sharply curtailing the use of filibusters in federal court nominations. By a

52–48 vote, with all of the 52 votes supplied by Democrats and three Democrats opposing the measure, the Senate voted to change its rules to allow federal district and circuit court and executive branch nominations be confirmed by a simple majority of senators. Supreme Court nominees would still require sixty votes, but in recent decades no Supreme Court nominee has been subject to a filibuster. Majority frustration over the ideological and partisan polarization in the Senate prompted the rules change (Kane and Branigan 2013).

Patterns of Conflict over Judicial Nominations

Because of the widely acknowledged policymaking role of federal courts, partisan and ideological Senate battles over nominees has now become commonplace. The number of federal appeals and district court nominees confirmed dropped from near 100 percent in the 1960s to below 50 percent in recent Congresses, particularly for appeals court nominees (Binder and Maltzman 2009, 3). Federal appeals court confirmation battles have grown with the decline in annual cases heard by the Supreme Court, from well over 150 in the 1960s to fewer than a hundred in the twenty-first century. With less Supreme Court review of appeals court decisions, the appeals courts have gained authority as final policymakers in many areas of law.

Partisan and ideological polarization, documented in our earlier chapters, and the rise of interest groups has made confirmation of appeals court nominees more difficult in recent decades. The incidence of votes that are party line—with all Democrats opposing all Republicans—and the frequency with which senators vote with their own party on roll calls share a common pattern with appeals court nominations. As party-line voting and party unity in voting increased in Congress, federal appeals court nomination success dropped and the length of the confirmation process increased. The more polarized partisan support for the president was in the Senate and among the public, the lower the level of appeals court confirmation success and the longer the process. The number of national interest groups had a strongly negative relationship with appeals nomination success and correlates positively with longer confirmation processes. The number of lower federal court nominations opposed by interest groups stood at zero until 1973 and then rose steadily to reach 33 percent by 2004 (Scherer 2005, 4). In all, partisan and ideological polarization and interest group proliferation raised the stakes in battles over judicial policymaking (Schier and Eberly, 135–36).

Appeals court nomination success was virtually certain until the late 1970s and early 1980s, when contestation began and rose to steadily higher levels by the twenty-first century. After 2000, the confirmation environment hardly resembles that of the 1950s and 1960s. Partisan and ideological polarization and less-certain confirmation outcomes have become the rule of the day. A causal analysis of appeals court nominations from 1947–2006 found that partisan and ideological polarization, measured as the absolute difference in the average ideology of each Senate party each year, had a strongly negative effect on both the length and success of appeals court nominations (Binder and Maltzman 2009, 92–96).

Two Ideological Supreme Court Rulings: Heller and Windsor

The stakes in judicial policymaking are frequently high, as in the following examples of the Supreme Court's policymaking regarding gun control and gay marriage. The Roberts Court has four conservative justices, four liberal justices, and one "swing" justice, the moderate conservative Anthony Kennedy. In recent years, both judicial conservatism and liberalism have triumphed in narrow 5-4 decisions, thanks to Kennedy's key vote. A recent landmark case on gun rights, *District of Columbia v. Heller* 554 U.S. 570 (2008), illustrates the "originalist" orientation of a 5-4 conservative majority. The case was brought to the Supreme Court by the District of Columbia, when the D.C. Circuit Court of Appeals overturned a D.C. law that prohibited the possession of handguns. The five majority votes came from the GOP appointees, including Kennedy. Justice Scalia's "originalist" majority opinion drew heavily on the history of the founders' intent in writing the text of the Second Amendment: "A well regulated militia being necessary to the security of a free state, the right of the people to keep and bear arms shall not be infringed." In the opinion, Scalia argued: "[T]here seems to us no doubt, on the basis of both text and history, that the Second Amendment conferred an individual right to keep and bear arms . . . it is not the role of this court to pronounce the Second Amendment extinct" (554 US 570 (2008) Opinion of the Court, 22, 64). In a dissent, Justice Stephen Breyer argued that changing circumstances made Scalia's focus on "original intent" inappropriate. Charging that this was a form of conservative judicial policymaking, he urged that the court defer to changing circumstances in interpreting the Second Amendment. Breyer's approach would require "careful identification of the relevant interests and evaluation of the law's effect on them" (554 US 570 [2008] Breyer dissenting, 41). For Breyer, changing circumstances would change the meaning of the Second Amendment—a "living constitution" approach.

The court moved in an emphatically liberal direction in its decision in *United States v. Windsor* 570 U.S. ___ (2013) concerning the constitutionality of the 1996 Defense of Marriage Act (DOMA), passed by a GOP Congress and signed by Democratic president Bill Clinton. The case involved Edith Windsor, married to Thea Speyer in Canada in 2007. When Speyer died, Windsor became liable for $363,053 in federal inheritance taxes that she would not have paid had their same-sex marriage been legally recognized by the federal government. Both the federal District Court and Circuit Court of Appeals hearing the case ruled DOMA unconstitutional and awarded Windsor full tax relief. The Supreme Court heard the case despite the fact that Windsor has already prevailed in a lower court.

By a 5-4 majority, the court interpreted the constitution as prohibiting federal bans on same-sex marriage, an example of a new, "living constitution" reinterpretation of the document. Along with the four Democratically-appointed justices, Justice Anthony Kennedy provided the swing vote and wrote the majority opinion. Kennedy argued that the Fifth Amendment's guarantee of "due process" to all citizens by the federal government voided any discrimination against gay marriage. This was a new application of the Fifth Amendment, reflecting what the majority saw to be changing social norms. The new majority argued opposition to same-sex marriage grew from an indefensible desire to harm homosexuals: "The principal purpose and the necessary effect of this law are to demean those persons who are in a lawful same-sex marriage. This requires the Court to hold . . . that DOMA is unconstitutional as a deprivation of the liberty of the person protected by the Fifth Amendment of the Constitution" (570 U.S. ___ [2013] Opinion of the Court, 25). Justice Samuel Alito, one of the four GOP appointees opposing the decision, argued on "originalist" grounds that the Constitution dictates nothing about same-sex marriage: "The Constitution does not speak to the issue of same-sex marriage. . . . [majority decision involves] arrogating to ourselves the power to decide a question that philosophers, historians, social scientists and theologians are better qualified to explore" (570 U.S. ___ [2013] Alito dissenting, 10, 14). In this case, an innovative constitutional interpretation prevailed over a conservative preference for constitutional originalism and traditional social arrangements.

As a result of the *Windsor* ruling, a wave of federal lower court decisions ensued holding that *Windsor* effectively legalized same-sex marriage. By mid-2014, four Federal Circuit Courts of Appeal had cited *Windsor* in ending gay-marriage bans in thirty-three states. The Supreme Court refused to review any of these decisions, despite appeals from gay-marriage opponents. The Sixth Circuit, however, in early November 2014, upheld gay-marriage bans in Kentucky, Tennessee, Michigan, and Ohio. This conflict between circuit courts brought about another Supreme Court decision on gay marriage, *Obergefell v. Hodges* 576 U.S. (2015). A sharply divided court ruled 5-4 in favor of a constitutional right to gay marriage with Justice Anthony Kennedy

delivering the majority opinion. Kennedy argued the Fourteenth Amendment guarantees of due process and equal protection to all citizens prohibited
states from discriminating in the awarding of marriage licenses on the basis
of sexual orientation.

The *Windsor* and *Heller* cases reveal a closely divided Supreme Court that
swings between liberal and conservative rulings, reflecting the broader ideological battles afflicting the country. The persistence of legal policymaking in
the state and national courts insures a continuing and large role for judges'
personal ideology in the decisions of American courts.

Conclusion

The rise of policymaking by the federal judiciary "is a change that emerged
prominently after World War II and then mushroomed after 1960" (Mackenzie 1996, 155). State courts followed the federal court lead. Consider the many
areas of policy directed and controlled by federal and state courts at present,
with most of this expanded jurisdiction resulting in the last fifty years. These
include criminal justice (police searches, a right to a lawyer in a criminal trial,
the right to be apprised of one's rights when arrested); reproductive freedom
(abortion, birth control); prayer in school and other church/state issues; affirmative action in hiring, promotion, firing, and university admissions; ter-
rorist detainment and treatment; the racial composition of elementary and
secondary schools and other controversies regarding discrimination concerning race, gender, and sexual orientation.

The federal courts also hold great sway over the economy by determining the
appropriate powers of Congress to "regulate interstate and foreign commerce"
under the Constitution. They also now determine the rules for the apportionment of legislative districts for state legislatures and the House of Representatives and the rules for funding federal legislative and presidential campaigns.
Furthermore, Congress, beginning in the 1960s, created many regulatory laws
concerning consumer protection, racial and gender discrimination, environmental protection, and disability access that depend on litigation in federal
court for thorough enforcement. "Whether we like it or not . . . court judges
are policymakers and litigation is a form of policymaking" (Barnes 2009, 108).

Accompanying broader policymaking power was the emergence of federal
judicial confirmations as ideological battlefields. Nancy Scherer summarizes
the steps that led to this outcome. First, political parties became dominated
by issue activists, ending the patronage basis of judicial selection and insert-
ing ideological concerns into the selection process. This led to presidents,
beginning with Johnson and Nixon, using ideological litmus tests in judicial

appointments, and prompted interest groups to form and make judicial confirmations the ground of ideological warfare. Both parties in the Senate began to obstruct confirmation of unacceptable nominees and at times the confirmation process became the locus of sensational political conflict, as in the Bork and Thomas confirmation hearings (Scherer 2004, 195–95). The warfare seems an enduring feature of America's ideological politics because it is the product of "effective conservative mobilization without significant displacement of liberalism" (Teles 2008, 274).

Federal and state courts since 1960 have effectively "judicialized politics." They "have been increasingly able and willing to impose substantive limits on the power of legislative institutions . . . have increasingly become places where substantive policy is made" and "have been increasingly willing to regulate the conduct of political activity itself—by . . . interest groups, political parties, and both elected and appointed officials" (Ferejohn 2002, 41). The courts' new power seems here to stay.

This is not to say that the judiciary runs every aspect of our political system. They have limited agenda power, in that they must wait for a dispute to be brought before them by others before a policy judgment can be made. Past precedents also bind them, and overturning a prior precedent, as the Supreme Court notably did in *Brown*, is a major, rare, and controversial event. Courts also must depend on legislatures and executives to comply with their decisions. In one notable case in 1985, *Immigration and Naturalization Service v. Chadha* 462 U.S. 919, the Supreme Court produced a sweeping decision invalidating hundreds of congressional laws that was ignored by both Congress and the president. That court voided the legislative veto, statutory language allowing Congress by a vote of a committee, one chamber, or both chambers to block a presidential action. In response, the national legislature and executive agreed to continue observing most forms of legislative veto because they found them mutually convenient (Fisher 2005).

If courts do not make policy with impunity, the new judicial system that evolved in the 1960s and 1970s gave courts more policymaking clout than ever before in American history. The question of democratic accountability is troublesome in this regard. No federal judges are subject to the voters and few state judges encounter truly competitive elections to remain in office. If judges effectively have lifetime appointments and make policy, are they operating democratically in such policymaking? As a leading text on American courts puts it: "In a democracy broad matters of public policy are, at least in theory, presumed to be left to the elected representatives of the people—not to judicial appointees with life terms. In principle, U.S. judges are not supposed to make policy, but in practice they cannot help but do so to some extent" (Carp, Stidham, and Manning 2011, 31). A key consequence is that legal professionals with ideological agendas now determine much policy previously decided by popular participation in elections. With courts, a result is "a diminished systemwide ability to construct proper foundations of popular support for new policy initiatives" (Mackenzie 1996, 159).

Federal and state court policymaking is another triumph of ideological governance. It is well entrenched because it is supported by interest groups of the left and right, the many ideological activists populating both major parties. Compliant senators respond to kindred activists and interest groups by making federal judicial confirmations an ideological and partisan battle zone. Conservatives argue for judicial "restraint," meaning a more conservative turn in court policymaking. Liberals, in contrast, seek judicial activism for "social justice" promoting a liberal direction. Everyone involved knows the courts make much important policy. Most of the public, however, is not involved. The courts' ideological governance reinforces many Americans' distrustful distance from their rulers.

References

Administrative Office of the U.S. Courts. 2012. "Civil Cases Commenced, by Nature of Suit, during the 12-Month Periods Ending September 30, 2007 through 2011." Table C-2A. http://www.uscourts.gov/uscourts/Statistics/JudicialBusiness/2011/appendices/C02ASep11.pdf (accessed May 31, 2012).

Alliance for Justice. 2011. *The State of the Judiciary: President Obama and the 111th Congress.* Washington, DC: Alliance for Justice.

Barnes, Jeb. 2009. "U.S. District Courts, Litigation, and the Policy-Making Process." In Mark C. Miller, ed., *Exploring Judicial Politics*, 97–109. Oxford: Oxford University Press.

Bell, Laura Cohen. 2002. *Warring Factions: Interest Groups, Money, and the New Politics of Senate Confirmation.* Columbus: Ohio State University Press.

Binder, Sarah H., and Forrest Maltzman. 2009. *Advice and Dissent: The Struggle to Shape the Federal Judiciary.* Washington, D.C.: Brookings Institution.

Brace, Paul, Melinda Gann Hall, and Laura Langer. 2001. "State Supreme Courts in State Politics." *Politics and Policy Quarterly* 1:81–108.

Brown v. Board of Education of Topeka 347 U.S. 483 (1954) and 349 U.S. 294 (1955).

Carp, Robert A., Ronald Stidham, and Kenneth L. Manning. 2011. *The Judicial Process in America*, 8th ed. Washington, DC: Congressional Quarterly Press.

District of Columbia v. Heller, 550 U.S. 570 (2008).

Dungworth, Terrence, and Nicholas M. Pace. 1990. *Statistical Overview of Civil Litigation in the Federal Courts.* Washington DC: Rand Corporation and Institute for Civil Justice.

Emmert, Craig F., and Carol Ann Traut. 1992. "State Supreme Courts, State Constitutions, and Judicial Policymaking." *Justice System Journal* 16:37–48.

Epstein, Lee, William M. Landes, and Richard A. Posner. 2013. *The Behavior of Federal Judges: A Theoretical and Empirical Study of Rational Choice.* Cambridge, MA: Harvard University Press.

Farhang, Sean. 2010. *The Litigation State: Public Regulation and Private Lawsuits in the U.S.* Princeton, NJ: Princeton University Press.

Federalist Society. 2012. "About Us." http://www.fed-soc.org/aboutus/ (accessed May 31, 2012).

Feeley, Malcolm M., and Edward L. Rubin. 2000. *Judicial Policymaking and the Modern State.* Cambridge: Cambridge University Press.

Ferejohn, John. 2002. "Politicizing Law." *Law and Contemporary Problems* 65 (3): 41–68.

Fisher, Louis. 2005. *Legislative Vetoes After Chadha.* Washington DC: Congressional Research Service.

Hirschl, Ran. 2008. "The Judicialization of Politics." In Keith E. Whittington, R. Daniel Kelemen, and Gregory A. Caldeira, eds., *The Oxford Handbook of Law and Politics,* 119–41. Oxford: Oxford University Press.

Horowitz, Donald L. 1977. *The Courts and Social Policy.* Washington, D.C.: Brookings Institution.

In re *Marriage Cases,* 183 P.3d 384 (Cal. 2008).

Jacob, Herbert. 1984. *Justice in America: Courts, Lawyers and the Judicial Process.* New York: Scott Foresman.

Judgepedia. 2013. "Political Outlook of State Supreme Court Justices." http://judgepedia.org/Political_outlook_of_State_Supreme_Court_Justices (accessed November 26, 2013).

Kagan, Robert A. 2001. *Adversarial Legalism: The American Way of Law.* Cambridge, MA: Harvard University Press.

Kane, Paul, and William Branigin. 2013. "Reid, Democrats Trigger 'Nuclear' Option; Eliminate Most Filibusters on Nominees." *Washington Post.* November 21. http://www.washingtonpost.com/politics/senate-poised-to-limit-filibusters-in-party-line-vote-that-would-alter-centuries-of-precedent/2013/11/21/d065cfe8-52b6-11e3-9fe0-fd2ca728e67c_story_1.html (accessed November 26, 2013).

Lawrence, Susan E. 1990. *The Poor in Court: The Legal Services Program and Supreme Court Decision Making.* Princeton, NJ: Princeton University Press.

Lieberman, Jethro K. 1981. *The Litigious Society.* New York: Basic Books.

Mackenzie, G. Calvin. 1996. *The Irony of Reform: Roots of American Political Disenchantment.* Boulder, CO: Westview Press.

Obergefell v. Hodges 576 U.S. (2015).

Roe v. Wade 410 U.S. 113 (1973).

Scherer, Nancy. 2005. *Scoring Points: Politicians, Activists, and the Lower Federal Court Appointment Process.* Stanford, CA: Stanford University Press.

Schier, Steven E., and Todd E. Eberly. 2013. *American Government and Popular Discontent.* New York: Routledge.

Segal, Jeffrey A., and Harold J. Spaeth. 2002. *The Supreme Court and the Attitudinal Model Revisited.* Cambridge: Cambridge University Press.

Silverstein, Gordon. 2009. *Law's Allure: How Law Shapes, Constrains, Saves, and Kills Politics.* Cambridge: Cambridge University Press.

Sunstein, Cass R., David Schkade, Lisa M. Ellman, and Andres Sawicki. 2006. *Are Judges Political? An Empirical Analysis of the Federal Judiciary.* Washington, DC: Brookings Institution.

Swann v. Charlotte Mecklenburg Board of Education 42 U.S. 1 (1971).

Teles, Steven M. 2007. "Conservative Mobilization against Entrenched Liberalism." In Paul Pierson and Theda Skocpol, eds., *The Transformation of American Politics: Activist Government and the Rise of Conservatism*, 160–88. Princeton, NJ: Princeton University Press.

———. 2008. *The Rise of the Conservative Legal Movement: The Battle for Control of the Law*. Princeton, NJ: Princeton University Press.

United States v. Windsor, 570 U.S. ____ (2013).

University of California Davis v. Bakke 438 U.S. 265 (1978).

Wilhelm, Teena. 2007. "The Policymaking Role of State Supreme Courts in Education Policy." *Legislative Studies Quarterly* 32:309–32.

Wolf, Richard. 2013. "Obama Tilts Federal Judiciary Back Toward Democrats." *USA Today*. November 1. http://www.usatoday.com/story/news/politics/2013/10/31/obama-judges-democrat-republican-senate/3286337/ (accessed November 26, 2013).

Ziegler, John C. 2003. "Historic Wyatt Case Ends." Alabama Department of Mental Health and Mental Retardation. December 8. http://www.mh.state.al.us/admin/downloads/MediaCenterDocuments/PR_31208_HistoricWyattCaseEnds.asp (accessed May 31, 2012).

7

Ideology's Impact on American Politics

A MERICA'S POLITICS HAVE BECOME INCREASINGLY IDEOLOGICAL in recent years. The reasons for this are several. Higher education levels have increased the sophistication of the American public, resulting in more citizens possessing higher levels of constraint, or predictable and logically interlinked views about politics. Constraint is a central trait of ideological thinking. People with ideological views trend to be more politically active. It is no surprise, then, that channels of political activity are filled with ideological citizens. We noted earlier how "party sorting" has accompanied America's more ideological politics. Democrats and Republicans increasingly sort themselves into liberal and conservative ideological camps. Liberal Republicans and conservative Democrats gradually are becoming as scarce as hula hoops and cassette tapes, to mention two once-widespread relics of the past.

In chapter 2, we explained how the dominant liberal–conservative dichotomy in governance and among political activists fails to adequately represent the views of many Americans. In particular, populists, who are economically liberal and socially conservative, and libertarians, who are economically conservative and socially liberal, don't fit the dichotomy well. They, along with moderates, don't fit easily into the now heavily liberal Democratic and heavily conservative Republican parties. Nor does the liberal–conservative dichotomy adequately represent the variety of orientations evident in our fifty state governments. Some states are true liberal blue and conservative red, but many display a mixed tendency. After the 2014 elections, eighteen states have control of their governments split between Democrats and Republicans.

The presidency has become an important institution for perpetuating and extending ideological politics. The presidential nomination process is dominated by liberal Democratic and conservative Republican activists, producing nominees who are very much in line with party ideology. George W. Bush and Barack Obama reflected well the ideological "conventional wisdom" of their parties and governed accordingly. Both often operated in a "party government" fashion by forming partisan coalitions to enact national policy. Both appointed federal judges and Supreme Court justices whose orientations fit the ideological mainstreams of their political parties. Over time, their partisan and ideological approaches helped to decrease the popularity of their presidencies. In response, they resorted to unilateral actions and to appeals to their partisan "bases." This inevitably raised the ire of rival partisans who found their ideological orientations and actions increasingly difficult to bear over time. A rancorous national politics has been the result.

Similarly ideological state leaders, such as conservative Republican Wisconsin governor Scott Walker, found themselves constantly involved in comparable ideological warfare in their states. Walker during his first term survived a recall election—a procedure in the state constitution allowing voters to remove an officeholder in the middle of his term by popular vote—and won a narrow reelection victory in 2014. His opponents were state liberals and their interest group allies, teachers, and public employee unions.

Congressional primaries in recent years have produced reliably liberal Democratic and reliably conservative Republican nominees in most districts. Once elected, the two parties have found very little common ground in the House and Senate. The majority party in each chamber has ruled in a "party government" fashion, according the minority party little legislative power. So little common ground now exists that maintaining the ongoing operations of national government has been a continuing struggle. Chapter 5 detailed the lengthy conflict between the parties leading to a government shutdown in October 2013. Occasional shutdowns have occurred since 1995, when a new conservative Republican Congress confronted Democratic president Bill Clinton. Merely keeping the federal government financially operating becomes a central ground of ideological warfare between the parties. The ability of lawmakers to negotiate and compromise has deteriorated greatly. Polarization on Capitol Hill seems here to stay.

A particularly controversial forum of ideological policymaking is that of the federal and state courts. The old tradition of "norm enforcement" of established laws has given way increasingly to judicial policymaking, in which judges impose their own ideological vision through their court decisions. Presidents and many governors in recent years have used informal "litmus tests" for selecting judicial nominees, thus insuring that the courts are stocked with judges who have an explicit ideological profile to their legal behavior. The courts, once somewhat removed from partisan and ideological warfare, now are important national and state policymaking venues. Frequent headlines record a new policy deriving from the ideological convictions of judges and justices.

Policy Government or Consensus Government?

Our more ideological politics now resemble what the authors of the doctrine of "responsible party government" advocated decades ago.[1] This group of re-formers suggested that democratic government requires political parties that (1) make policy commitments to the electorate, (2) are willing and able to carry them out when in office, (3) develop alternatives to government policies when out of office, and (4) differ sufficiently to "provide the electorate with a proper range of choice between alternatives of action" (Committee on Political Parties 1950, 1). They thus come to define a political party as "an association of broadly like-minded voters seeking to carry out common objectives through their elected representatives" (Committee on Political Parties 1950, 66). Parties should be grounded in common ideological commitments, and above all, function to fulfill those commitments. In this view, the electorate at large—not merely political activists—is assumed to be ideologically motivated to hold policy positions. Officeholders thus should pursue public mandates for ideological agendas.

Advocates of this approach hold the ideas animating the platforms at the national party conventions should command the national agenda. That way, our politics center on distinct and competing ideological visions of the two parties and their activists. These platforms must make policy that will be en-forced on national, state, and local levels by means of party discipline—that is, getting rid of party officeholders who disagree. A result is ideologically driven campaigns, elections, and governance.

In this approach, the weaknesses of parties and the disabilities of governments are seen as stemming from failure to develop and support satisfactory programs of public policy. Political scientists Nelson Polsby and Aaron Wildavsky termed this approach "a theory of *policy government.*" It holds "that the choices pro-vided by the two party system are valuable to the American people in proportion to their definition in terms of public policy" (Committtee on Political Parties 1950, 15). Policy government grows from and sustains an ideological politics.

Yet there is an alternative way to think of the proper role of political parties and governmental institutions. That approach requires that parties and gov-erning institutions first and foremost undertake the minimization of conflict between contending interests and social forces. This approach, also originally defined by Nelson W. Polsby and Aaron Wildavsky, advocates not ideological policy government but instead *consensus government.* In this view, political parties and governing institutions are mechanisms for furthering adjustment

and compromise among the various interests in society to prevent severe social conflict. Opponents of ideologically-based policy government hold that
"the general welfare is achieved by harmonizing and adjusting group interest" (Herring 1965, 327). Supporters of consensus government see parties
and governing institutions as "agents for compromise" and view the current
polarization of American politics as a big impediment to that.

Conflict within and between parties may be good for them and for the nation. Conflict can invigorate discussion and enlighten the public about the
bases of party differences. But much depends on the extent to which discussion quickly polarizes groups that have strong interests that are already so well
formed that the search for creative solutions disappears. That becomes much
more likely as America's politics and governance become more ideological.

We have seen that party activists and, to a lesser but meaningful extent,
legislators have become ideologically more coherent. This has occurred by
evolution: northern liberal Republicans have moved into the Democratic
Party and conservative southern Democrats into the Republican Party. Presidents now reliably reflect the dominant ideology of their political party. The
increasing uniformity and importance of party ideology has not been good
for the parties, governance, or the nation.

Recent examples abound. Several policies implemented by the Bush and
Obama administrations proved unpopular with voters, demonstrating that
neither narrow (Bush) nor comfortable (Obama) election victories confer
broad mandates to execute a comprehensive issue agenda. Bush's popularity
ratings dropped as the U.S. war in Iraq suffered significant setbacks. In 2006,
voters communicated their disapproval of his performance in office by turning
control of both houses of Congress over to the opposition Democrats. Congressional Republicans suffered particularly heavy losses in liberal and moderate districts in the North, where voters registered their strong objections to the
policies of the ruling GOP by defeating even centrist Republican incumbents.

Similar results in 2008 ushered in Democratic dominance of Congress and
the presidency under Barack Obama. In turn, Obama's pursuit of a liberal
policy agenda increased the electoral vulnerability of moderate Democrats
from the South and West who, in adopting policy positions, faced an unap-
petizing choice between satisfying either their party leaders or their constitu-
ents. Obama's declining popularity led to heavy losses for these Democrats
in the 2010 and 2014 midterm elections, giving control of Congress to the
Republican Party in 2015 while further increasing the extent of ideological
polarization and partisan rancor within Congress.

Bush and Obama both pursued ideological agendas in their approach to
the federal judiciary. The presidents unswervingly appointed individuals to
the federal courts who upheld the ideological convictions of their party's
activists. This served to make the federal courts even more of an ideological

battlefield as Bush's conservative appointees battled with Obama's liberals at all levels of the national judiciary.

Are parties, presidents, and legislators that take relatively extreme positions more "responsible" or "accountable" to the generally moderate and ideologically inconsistent American electorate than a politics that allows for greater flexibility on issues? Governance that reinforces party polarization risk offering voters a clear choice—but between two equally unpalatable options. To a large extent, advocates of policy government have succeeded in implementing their goals, but the results may have proven less popular—and less conducive to well-functioning government—than they foresaw.

As we have seen in previous chapters, most voters in the United States are not very ideologically oriented. They do not seek to create or to adopt systems of thought in which issues are related to one another in some highly consistent manner. Caring about more than one value, sometimes they prefer a strong government here and a weak one there, or want just not to decide at the present time. Thus voters can hardly be said to transmit strong preferences for a uniform stream of particular policies by electing candidates to public office.

The parties, Congress and the presidency, and the federal courts have been greatly strengthened in their capacities to provide ideological advocacy and weakened in their abilities to provide intermediation or later to facilitate implementation in the political system, that is, governing. Consensus among the currently dominant group of ideological activists is now achieved at the expense of increasing dissension within government. Long-standing government responsibilities become compromised. Partisan approaches became more ideologically consistent while government finds it increasingly difficult to relate revenues to expenditures in many states and in the national government. Budget deficits grew steadily worse during the George W. Bush and early Obama presidencies, as partisan advocacy of tax cuts (for Bush) or spending programs (for Obama) triumphed over the more difficult governance problem of budget management.

Issue advocacy is strengthened and governance impeded because the rules of the game offer incentives to party leaders and candidates who are able to attract personal followings on an ideological basis. What is lost is a capacity to deliberate, weigh competing demands, and compromise so that a variety of differing interests each gain a little. This loss would not be so great if the promise of policy government—to select sound programs and implement them successfully—were likely to be fulfilled in performance. But, on the record so far, this is pretty doubtful.

It is doubtful because for many of the problems discussed in political campaigns—economic growth, crime, poverty, terrorism—there are no known, sure-fire solutions. And even if we knew what to do about more of our problems, it is improbable, given the ways in which various forces in our society and responsibilities in our constitution are arranged, that presidents, Congress, our courts, or state governments alone could deliver on their promises. Policy government might improve the legitimacy of government if it increased the effectiveness of programs, but the insensitivity of its advocates to the need for consensus makes that unlikely. Under these circumstances, sound policy, consensus, and constructive intermediation are unlikely to result.

The Decline of Parties as Intermediaries

Two changes account for the decline in the vital function of intermediation by political parties. First, many candidates for state and national office now need no longer build up a mosaic of alliances with interest groups and party leaders. Instead, through the miracle of the mass media, candidates can reach every home and touch every heart and claim the allegiance of followers based on ideological or stylistic affinity rather than concrete bargains. The 2008 Obama campaign, touting an attractive "hope and change" pitch, is the preeminent example of successful "affinity politics." This is the first sense in which our politics have been diminished in their capacity to mediate between the desires of ordinary citizens and the policies of government: candidates no longer need parties to reach voters personally.

In a second sense, political parties are losing the capacity to mediate between leaders and followers because primary elections leave little room for a bargaining process to occur. Complex preferences are impossible to express in primary elections straightforwardly through the ballot. Thus a candidate who is acceptable to a sizable majority but is the first choice of only a few systematically loses out under the current primary-driven rules to candidates who might be unacceptable to most voters but secure in their control over a middle-sized fraction (20 to 30 percent, depending on how many candidates play the game) of first-choice votes.

These changes have helped create government that often operates on false premises. The premises on which policy government is based are untrue. Most people do not want parties, candidates, and political leaders that make extreme appeals by taking issue positions far from the desires of the bulk of the citizenry. Perhaps people feel safer if their parties give them a choice, but they do not want losing to be a catastrophe. This may be why they see no great difficulty in voting for a president or governor of one party and a Congress or state legislature of another.

After a few decades of severe internal difficulty, when confidence in virtually all national institutions has slumped, the need for consensus-building in American politics seems clearer than ever. Can a very large multiracial, multiethnic, multireligious, multiregional, multiclass nation such as the United States sustain itself when its main political actors—political parties and officeholders in governing institutions—strive to exclude rather than include, to sharpen rather than dull the edge of controversy?

It is even doubtful that the recent rise of ideological advocacy leads to a more principled politics. If principles are precepts that must not be violated, when contrary principles are firmly embedded in the programs of opposing parties, one person's principles necessarily become another's fighting words. A few principles, such as those enshrined in the Bill of Rights, may be helpful—indeed essential—in establishing boundaries beyond which governmental action may not go. But too many principles thwart the cooperative government required by the design of the Constitution. As being a Democrat increasingly requires adherence to litmus-tested liberal positions and a Republican to litmus-tested conservative positions, cross-cutting cleavages—organizing people who support one another on some issues while opposing on others—are bound to diminish. With officeholders opposing each other on more issues, and with more issues defined as moral issues, political passions are liable to rise. And so will negative campaigning and popular disapproval of government and of politicians.

Ideological Politics versus the American Constitution

The American founders did not design a system to encourage and enhance an ideological politics. Their separation of powers between the executive and legislature aimed to slow the pace of government and enhance deliberation. As James Madison put it in Federalist #10, the duty of elected representatives was to "refine and enlarge public views by passing them through the medium of a chosen body of citizens, whose wisdom may best discern the true interest of their country, and whose patriotism and love of justice will be least likely to sacrifice it to temporary or partial considerations." Rigid ideological agendas are the very definition of Madison's "partial considerations." Discovering the "true interest of the country" is only likely to occur through careful deliberation and, ultimately, compromise. By separating powers so elaborately, the founders sought to create a system in which compromise and intermediation would facilitate consensus government. It's no wonder that ideological politics function so poorly in a constitutional system designed to prevent any one ideological agenda from dominating the councils of government.

Though a politics without policies would be empty, politics fixated on only a narrow band of policies is dangerous. Without the desire to win elections, not at any cost but as a leading motive, there is no reason for politicians to pay attention to the people who vote. Winning requires a widespread appeal. Thus the desire to win can lead to moderation, to appeals to diverse groups in the electorate, and to efforts to bring many varied interests together. This is why we prefer a politics of consensual intermediation, a politics of ideological advocacy.

Parties of ideological advocacy do not sustain themselves well in government. They fail to assist political leaders in mobilizing consent for the policies they adopt, and this widens the gap between campaign promises and the performance of government. This, we believe, was the fate of the Republican Party during George W. Bush's time in the White House and the Democratic Party during Barack Obama's presidency.

Ideological politics is an enemy of our constitutional order. Our system of widely scattered powers separated in national government and divided and shared between the national and state governments was not designed to facilitate quick approval of sweeping ideological agendas. It's unlikely our constitutional order will change anytime soon. It still commands the allegiance of a large majority of Americans (Herrnson and Weldon 2014). Given that, it will only serve to frustrate the ideological designs of the executives, legislators, judges, and party activists who seek to push their agenda through our unwelcoming institutions.

Our nation's founders wanted governance to reflect popular opinion by requiring extensive deliberation among contrasting viewpoints before government acts. An ideological politics shuns such deliberation. For the ideological citizens, the truth is known and discussion of it is far from vital. We can only expect governmental performance and popular legitimacy to improve when consensus government replaces the newly ascendant policy government— when deliberation and compromise replace attempts by ideological activists and power holders to impose their preferences on their fellow citizens.

References

Committee on Political Parties, American Political Science Association. 1950. *Toward a More Responsible Two-Party System*. Washington D.C.: American Political Science Association.

Herring, Pendleton. 1965. *The Politics of Democracy: American Parties in Action*. Revised Edition. New York: W. W. Norton.

Herrnson, Paul, and Kathleen Weldon. 2014. "The Public and Proposed Constitutional Amendments: We Love You, You're Perfect, Now Change." *Huffington Post*. September 15. http://www.huffingtonpost.com/paul-herrnson/the-public-and-proposed-c_b_5812708.html (accessed December 3, 2015).

Polsby, Nelson W., Aaron Wildavsky, Steven E. Schier, and David A. Hopkins. 2012. *Presidential Elections: Strategies and Structures of American Politics*, 13th ed. Lanham, MD: Rowman & Littlefield.

Note

1. Much of the analysis in the following pages derives from Polsby et al. (2012, chaps. 6 and 7).

Index

abortion: conservative view of, 3, *4*, 5, 6, 10, 12, 27, 36, *37*; debate about, 16, 34, 36–39, *38*, 96; liberal view of, 3, *4*, 5, 7, 15, 30, 32, 36, 37, *37*, 38; *Roe v. Wade*, 29, 36, 38

Abramowitz, Alan, 36, 51–52, 53, 54, 55, 61

administrative tools, for ideological ends, 79–80

advocacy, 118, 134, 137, 138; congressional, 70, 90, 133, 135, 136; issue, 135; presidential, 66, 74, 78, 114

affirmative action, 14

Affordable Care Act, 13, 66, 70, 74, 78, 80, 88, 102

Afghanistan, 65, 70, 74, 80, 83

African Americans, 18, 29, 94–95; civil rights of, 14, 34–35; ideology of, 5, *17*

Alliance for Justice, 120

America: ideology in, 24–28; partisanship in, 29–30

American Bar Association, 118

American Civil Liberties Union, 120

American Enterprise Institute, 73

American Federation of Labor-Congress of Industrial Organizations, 18

American ideological classifications, *28*

American media, American political ideology in, 2–3

American National Election Studies (ANES), 25–26, 32, 33, 56

American political ideology, in American media, 2–3

American Political Science Association (APSA), 89–90, 93

American politics. *See* contemporary American politics; ideology, in American politics

American public. *See* ideology, in the American public

Americans for Democratic Action, 18

American states. *See* political division, in American states

The American Voter (Campbell, Converse, Miller, Stokes), 29, 30, 31, 32

ANES. *See* American National Election Studies

APSA. *See* American Political Science Association

Articles of Confederation, 44

About the Authors

Steven E. Schier is Dorothy H. and Edward C. Congdon Professor of Political Science at Carleton College, where he has taught the past thirty years. He also directs the Carleton in Washington program, an off-campus term of study he founded in 1983. Schier is the author or coauthor of seven books, including *Panorama of a Presidency: How George W. Bush Acquired and Spent His Political Capital* (2008), which won an "outstanding academic book" award from Choice magazine. He has edited six books, including *The Postmodern President: Bill Clinton's Legacy in U.S. Politics* (2000) and *High Risk and Big Ambition: The Presidency of George W. Bush* (2004). Schier has written about Obama's election in his recent book *The American Elections of 2008* (2008), coedited with Janet Box-Steffensmeier. His most recent works are the edited volumes *Ambition and Division: Legacies of the George W. Bush Presidency* (2009), *Transforming America: Barack Obama in the White House* (2011), and the thirteenth edition of *Presidential Elections: Strategies and Structures of American Politics*, coauthored with Nelson W. Polsby, Aaron Wildavsky, and David A. Hopkins (2011).

Todd E. Eberly is an assistant professor of political science and coordinator of public policy studies at St. Mary's College of Maryland. Before joining the St. Mary's College, Eberly was a senior analyst with the Hilltop Institute, a health policy firm based at the University of Maryland Baltimore County (UMBC). He was recently named one the most influential voices in Maryland politics by *Campaigns and Elections* magazine.

67597421R00097

Made in the USA
San Bernardino, CA
24 January 2018